The Best Selling Coac

Written by a sister and brother team with 35 years of combined experience, this book demystifies business development and offers a simple and highly effective method of selling for business coaches and consultants.

Selling professional services, particularly for new or aspiring consultants, can seem daunting and distasteful. This book shows that it doesn't need to be this way and, using a four-stage process, shows coaches how to first build their confidence and go on to locate, connect and meet desirable clients, virtually or in person. This book guides readers through asking for the sale and keeping control of the business relationship as it develops. Complete with email and letter templates and LinkedIn strategies, many chapters also link to an online course which gives access to downloadable materials such as professionally designed PDFs suitable for workshops, presentations and coaching sessions.

Current, new and aspiring business coaches, as well as postgraduate coaching students, will welcome this guide to solving the top issues most people face in this sector: finding new clients, building your client base and winning work.

Rebecca Bonnington was born in Banbury and raised in Manchester from the age of one. Her down-to-earth, no-nonsense approach to business coaching and consulting has served her clients well over the past 16 years. She lives in Edinburgh with her husband, youngest daughter and two dogs. Her two older children live close by. She's the CEO and Co-Founder of Tricres and describes herself as the business coach's coach.

Nick Davies began his first business at the age of 19 and has since started four others, as well as having periods of being employed in retail and field sales. He studied law as a mature student, being called to the Bar of England and Wales at 32. Since 2007 Nick has been delivering communication skills training across the globe and frequently speaks at international conferences. He is a visiting lecturer at The Smurfit Business School, University College, Dublin.

The Best Selling Coach

Business Development for Business Coaches, Consultants and Advisors

Rebecca Bonnington
and Nick Davies

For Tom

Best Wishes

19 Nov 2025

Routledge
Taylor & Francis Group
NEW YORK AND LONDON

Designed cover image: Lauren Jones

First published 2025
by Routledge
605 Third Avenue, New York, NY 10158

and by Routledge
4 Park Square, Milton Park, Abingdon, Oxon, OX14 4RN

Routledge is an imprint of the Taylor & Francis Group, an informa business

ISBN: 9781032991214 (hbk)
ISBN: 9781032991207 (pbk)
ISBN: 9781003602422 (ebk)

DOI: 10.4324/9781003602422

Typeset in Galliard Pro
by codeMantra

Contents

Foreword

About This Book

This book's about selling and developing business.

This book has been written by Rebecca Bonnington and her older and far better-looking brother, Nick Davies.

It's opinionated.

You'll agree with some of it and disagree with others. We don't care. Frankly, your opinion of us is none of our business.

It's personal. What follows is written from our point of view, founded on over a combined 60 years of business experience. It's full of stories and anecdotes: our stories and anecdotes, things that we've done, written, said and experienced.

There's a lot of stuff about winning business in the professional service sector. That's because We've sold lots of training, coaching and consultancy services to this market. Rebecca has used these techniques in all kinds of sectors, including construction, architecture, IT, finance, manufacturing and tech. Nick was once a lawyer and likes lawyers and Rebecca has an MSc in Coaching so she likes all kinds of businesses.

This is just one book about selling: it's not intended to be the definitive guide.

If this is the only book about selling you read, you're being silly. There are loads out there so go and read them. Read lots but understand this; the only way you'll actually get good at selling is by doing rather than reading. You can read about how to swim, but if you don't get in the pool, you'll always be rubbish.

Anyone can read it. However, we really intended this book to be aimed at those of you who do not regard yourselves as salespeople but find yourself having to develop business as part of your existing or hoped-for life as a coach or consultant.

The chances are you've accrued many years of experience in your field. You have learned a great deal and know a wide variety of people with the extensive network you've woven over the decades.

Whilst you are undoubtedly comfortably confident in your specialist arena, you either don't know where to start when it comes to developing business or sense your current efforts could be so much better!

You CAN learn this stuff. It's easy and we are here to show you what to do and how to best execute it. Relax. We really do know what we're doing.

You don't have to become like us. You just need to adopt and adapt what we know works to suit your personality and character.

We've written this book to encourage you to keep going as a business coach, consultant or advisor. To help you even more, we've added some online courses you can access via the handy QR codes you'll see at the end of some chapters. Once you purchase one of these courses (they're extremely good value for money) you get to keep them and use them as often as you wish.

For those of you who wish to become business coaches, you can learn more about our Kick Ass Culture Coach Training by visiting www.tricres.com.

Enjoy.

Why You Should Read This Book

Why you should read it and who will it benefit?

We recommend business coaches, consultants and advisors read this book. Throughout this book, we use business coaches as the example and most of those people are one-woman or one-man bands. We know many people in professional services work for larger organisations though. The content in this book is highly relevant for you too. Even though you may work in a large business, it's still you the clients are buying from. Your personality is what they engage with and they stick with you. So, you are in effect a mini-business within a business. You're likely to have targets too.

So, wherever you read 'business coach' think 'business professional' and enjoy.

Because by the end of it, you'll understand how to win more work, charge more for it and enjoy the life you've always wanted.

We know it works because people who have used our services tell us and above all it's how we've built our very successful businesses: we have the company accounts, to prove it!

Most of what we share is common sense. (However, common sense is sometimes not practically applied.) Having said that, one of the main themes running through this book concerns standing out from the crowd, which means that sometimes you need to step away from what Sir Ken Robinson referred to as...

"the tyranny of common sense".

What's different about this book?

There's no jargon. It gets straight to the point.

We talk plainly, in a straightforward and, sometimes, humorous way about sales and developing business.

We've created a book designed to be read from start to finish or be dipped into. Whilst it does make sense to begin at page one, it's quite OK to head straight for the chapter which most interests you.

Who We Are

Who are we?

"Who the heck is Nick Davies?"

I'm officially 'Nicholas Ian Davies', the name you'll find on my passport and driving license, but 'Nick' in everyday life.

I've been selling since 1986. I have started 5 businesses from scratch – the first, at 19 – 3 on my own and 2 with my sister!

After completing college, where I earned a National Diploma in Business and Finance with Travel and Tourism, I moved out of the family home and into my first rented house with my best mate and started a catering business: all in the same week.

On our first day, we sold 13 sandwiches but within a year had moved on to producing pre-packed ones, in a room in the back of a bakery we were renting and were knocking out 350 a day. However, the venture, whilst exciting, didn't work out and we went our separate ways.

After the sandwich episode I got a job selling ad space in a large business directory, which I did for a year before moving on to what turned out to be a number of sales roles with different firms, selling, office equipment, leasing agreements on fax machines, radio advertising, phone systems and water and air filters for the domestic market, those final two products via a multi-level marketing scheme, which resulted in me losing my house, car, credit cards and very nearly being declared bankrupt at the age of 26.

Following this rather humbling experience and huge fall from grace, I decided to become a barrister.

After six years of studying part-time, whilst selling shoes and handbags in a high-end retailer I finally gained my law degree and was called to the Bar of England and Wales.

I didn't like it one bit. So I left and moved my young family from Manchester to Edinburgh, where Rebecca and I started a recruitment consultancy. She recruited accountants and me, lawyers.

The business was successful and at its peak had 18 employees across 2 offices.

However, my legal clients began asking me if I could help develop their BD/selling and all-around communication skills, and that's how I ended up training and moving away from recruitment.

In January 2008 I went out alone, as a sole trader and began the business from the bottom up. Lots of telephone cold calls, countless meetings and goodness know how much shoe leather later I had built an employee-free, office-free, highly profitable lifestyle business, which was regularly generating £18,000 per month. My biggest month was £39,765! I was being flown across the globe business and first class to deliver training from West Virginia to New Zealand, staying in beautiful hotels, my clients paying for all of it! AND enjoying three months of holiday a year!

However, what working for ourselves has really given us is…time and the ability to live life on our terms, answerable to no one other than our clients. Doing what we want, when we want, which has allowed us to be actively involved parents, and able to attend school plays and sports days: a luxury many people in business sadly miss.

"Who the heck is Rebecca Bonnington?"

I took a different path from Nick. I studied hard at school so I could escape to university and read books. A degree in English Literature took me into the glamorous world of temp admin work. That's right, I started as an admin assistant in British Rail, working with 350 male, signal design engineers who were mainly from Yorkshire. Progressive, it was not.

I quickly rose to the heady rank of Manager, Level 1, only one of four females at a managerial grade and most definitely the youngest. I was told I'd been promoted too quickly and would not be promoted again for at least two years. Reader, I left.

1994 saw the start of my career in the recruitment industry. A fabulous and often maligned industry, which taught me how to sell, work well with people and understand human nature.

In 1999, at the tender age of 28, I started my first business. With a large mortgage, a young child and the main wage earner in the household, I thought it was a great idea to start my own recruitment business and leave the security of a large salary, pension, company car and share options.

With many twists and turns, I found myself in the world of leadership coaching. I'd had to close the recruitment business in the banking crash of 2008 and had retrained as a coach, using NLP (Neuro-Linguistic Programming) as the foundation for my practice.

In 2012 I gained a Master's Degree in Coaching and in 2018, persuaded my older brother, once again to join me in a business venture.

This book contains my insights into building a successful coaching and consulting business whilst raising three kids and running a household. I didn't go down the same route as Nick; I couldn't because I had three kids to raise, so my earnings were lower, my best month was December 2019, during which I billed £25,000 and turned over a solid £138k on my own. Not bad for four days a week.

Chapter 1

So You Want to Be a Business Coach and Consultant

The reality of what it's like.

There are numerous reasons why people choose to go it alone. Some are 'forced' into it through redundancy, others because they simply refuse to continue working in an unfulfilling job or career and some because they are excited about the possibility of becoming independently well-off and enjoying a life of abundance and freedom.

It's been our experience the majority of people wanting to become coaches and consultants with Tricres or on their own harbour the following worries:

- Not getting sufficient clients to pay you enough to pay the bills
- Picking the wrong people/organisation to train with and learn from
- Not having the skills to get set up and get going
- Not being the 'right fit' or having the 'right kind of experience' or qualification
- Not being qualified
- Not having the right support to keep going and be wildly successful

You don't need to know it all before getting started

Over the years we've met a good number of people wishing to work for themselves who've told us they don't feel confident promoting what they are offering without having an entire 'product' range or detailed knowledge of everything going on in their profession.

This is silly because in the case of the product range, you'll always be able to add one more thing and in the case of a knowledge-based service, there will always be more that you could learn!

Furthermore, we have spent years building and refining our training platform so you have instant access to everything from day one AND, more importantly, provide you with step-by-step guides on how to introduce it to prospective clients and then go on to work with them. We are holding your hand through your journey to becoming a successful coach and consultant.

DOI: 10.4324/9781003602422-1

Ups and Downs

There's no doubt about it, there are highs and lows when working for yourself: fortunately far more of the former rather than the latter!

If you are sick or have to care for a loved one, you won't get paid. Neither will you when on holiday.

On the other hand, you can have days off without having to notify anyone or make sure it's OK and, when on holiday, you can actually relax in the knowledge someone from the office is not going to ask you to 'just quickly jump on a call'.

What's more, because Rebecca and I have experienced these ups and downs, we've provided you with the information and content to make sure your coaching and consulting business follows a smoother and more even path!

Saying 'No'

The temptation, when you are responsible for generating your own income, is to say 'yes' to every offer of work that comes along. Don't!

If a client approaches you and asks you to spend half a day with their organisation for £500, and you oblige, it's then much harder to go back to them and ask for £1,500 because you've set the benchmark.

However, you might feel £166 per hour (£500 divided by 3 assuming half a day is 3 hours) is a decent amount compared to what most people earn an hour.

Indeed it is. But remember, your client is not paying you for an hour of your time, they are paying for the years of expertise you have accrued! They are paying for that knowledge and wisdom.

Be proud of your price. Know your worth. That insight or nugget of knowledge you take for granted could be the thing which saves or earns them tens of thousands of pounds or dollars, perhaps 100s of thousands!

Do not sell yourself short, tempting though it may be to accept the work.

If you're expensive you must be good.

We are all familiar with: 'You get what you pay for' and the coaching and consulting world is no different.

We perceive something more expensive must be better than the cheap alternative, and in virtually every case, that's true – watches, shoes, cars, property, luggage, food, holidays, hotels, toiletries, insurance policies, etc.

The danger, therefore, is if you charge too little, the perception is your offering is inferior to the coach and consultant who charges three times as much.

There is also a 'kudos' value; a kind of 'We are the sort of business which can afford the very best'

Imagine being an employee of an organisation in which the management team informs you that you are going to attend coaching to help improve your skills, and then to be told, "Yeah, we've found this coach for you. We shopped around and found the cheapest we could find! Isn't that great!" Wow! How Valued Do You Feel?

You have to log every expense and keep good records.

Nick was never that good at managing money until he ran his own business, which is when he suddenly became acutely aware of what he was spending and where!

In the beginning, money will be tight, unless you are blessed with a large pot of cash from an asset sale or redundancy payment.

You must get into the habit of logging all your expenditures and err on the side of caution when buying your business essentials, such as PC, laptop, software, etc.

You may want the very latest, most powerful, stunning-looking Apple computer, but the dull Dell from the local retail park will do just as well and save you a lot of money.

You may decide you are prepared to travel far and wide for the right assignment with the right client. Fair enough. Travel standard class. Travel at cheaper times. Perhaps driving or getting a coach or bus to your destination is the cheapest option.

Similarly with Accommodation

Nick admits he likes the privacy of a hotel and having his room refreshed for his return from a day's work. Others like the AirBNB route.

When we first started out we stayed in some down-at-heel places in London, which is where most of our business was. There were some really awful rooms! But it's all either of us could afford. Rebecca remembers one in particular near King's Cross Station in London. The room was so bad, she felt like she was in a prison cell. So you suck it up and get on with it until you are generating the income and can justify a bit more.

There's never a good time.

You won't get an argument from either Rebecca or myself about that!

Those of you who have kids will know it only too well!

But Ask Yourself, 'If Not Now, When?'

Let's be clear, you can put this off for as long as you want because there will always be an excuse. Wait until the weather is better, the kids are off school, once Christmas has gone, after the holiday, in the New Year, once the economy picks up/interests are more stable/lower, there's more market certainty/after the next election...and so the reasons go on!

Bottom line: If you are waiting for the 'perfect' conditions before you make that leap of faith you are going to be waiting forever... conditions are NEVER EVER going to be perfect.

Nick started his business in January 2008 just as the world economy was collapsing and banks were teetering on total collapse. To describe the timing as 'slightly off' would be a monumental understatement.

But that's what he did and he has no regrets – he went on to earn a great deal of money and enjoy an opulent lifestyle (for a bloke working alone).

We regret the things we did not do rather than those we did.

So true.

Going it alone is a big decision. It can also be a decision that's made for you. Whether it's redundancy, a change of family circumstances or the desire to simply work for yourself on your terms, the decision to become a coach and consultant can be a big one.

Or, in my case, it was a matter of being unemployable. After closing my recruitment business in 2008 (Nick had left in 2007), I found myself with two kids under 11 and a third one on the way. At nine months pregnant, no one would employ me so I decided to take six months off and consider my options.

Being a proud, independent woman, I did not want to rely on my husband's income so I set to work using my NLP skills to drum up business in the weight loss arena. It became clear very quickly I was not cut out for that, I didn't have the patience.

I considered getting a proper job in social work or teaching. Then I saw how much they earned and decided against it, I think the bureaucracy would have killed me anyway.

With childcare fixed for three days a week, I had enough time to develop clients for my fledgling leadership coaching practice. I contacted all my old clients and not one of them wanted me as a coach.

My mantra in recruitment had always been to 'follow the money'. I looked at the organisations that still had money and targeted them.

Nick talks about valuing yourself. During these early days, I was approached by a large law firm that wanted me to work with one of their clients on leadership and communication. I believe the topic was 'having difficult conversations'.

They asked me to do some work for one of their large clients – an international bank. I happily quoted a fee of £1,500 for the day and flew down to London to train a room full of their senior managers.

One of these people was particularly unpleasant and did not value the training at all. The rest were great.

The bank loved the work and asked me to come back to deliver more. I said I'd be delighted to and would be charging them £2,000 per day as this time I was including my travel and accommodation costs. Something, I'd not done before as I was doing 'a favour' for the law firm.

They did not come back to me. The law firm did though. They said they'd received fantastic feedback from their clients at the bank and wanted me to deliver the same course to their partners. Again, I said I'd be delighted to do that and the charge would be £1,500 as their offices were in my home town.

Their Head of Learning and Development was surprised I was proposing to charge for the work and told me he'd like it for free. Now, the paintings hanging on the wall of these law firm's offices cost more than most people earn in a year. I politely declined and never heard from them again.

A large public sector organisation got me into their offices to do a 'lunch and learn' for their team with the promise of more paid work. The lunch and learn was great and the paid work did not materialise.

I'd like you to answer some questions based on these stories.

- Have you ever been tempted to do things for free with the promise of more paid work?
- How did that work out? Did the paid work ever materialise?
- Have you ever delivered work to people who don't value what you do? Did you get any more work out of it or were you knocked down on price? How did that work out for you?

I'm guessing the outcomes of the above questions were not wholly positive.

Part of being mentally prepared for the world of coaching and consulting is knowing your own value. I didn't at first and it wasted a huge amount of time.

The moment I decided to work only with people who valued what I did meant I could charge accordingly and people were very happy to pay. They still are.

A Quick Note on Imposter Syndrome

Everyone has it. You're not alone. It doesn't make you special. Sorry to burst your bubble.

I've coached the most senior people in the biggest organisations you can imagine and they all feel like an imposter until they don't. The only people I've ever worked with who don't feel like an imposter are the sociopaths. They don't care about anything except themselves and have zero self-awareness, they think they're bloody brilliant at everything.

Reframe that feeling of being an imposter. Decide, instead to feel it and then use it as a way to improve your offering or get more practice.

Some people think imposter syndrome is unique to women. It's not. I've coached many men who feel it just as keenly as women, they don't talk about it as openly, but they feel it.

View that nervous, edgy, 'why me' feeling as 'this is normal' and 'I'll use it to improve' feeling.

If you're crippled by imposter syndrome to the point where you stop doing things, you need to seek help from a coach or therapist if it is really bad.

Last Work on Mental Preparedness

You will get rejected. People will say 'no' to you. Some people will never return your calls or your emails. You'll meet people with whom you get on well and you'll never get any work from them.

It's not you.

It's business.

Not everyone is ready to engage, not everyone has the time or the money, not everyone values what you do and not everyone likes you. This is a good thing. There are eight billion people on the planet and you do not want all of them to like you. That would be horrible and quite exhausting.

In the same way, your pet dog likes Bruno the Boxer down the road more than Penelope the Poodle next door, some people like you more than other people and those are the people you want to work with.

Accept it because you can't change it. If it's a 'no' then say to yourself 'next' and move on.

Being Financially Prepared

Make sure you have three to six months worth of money to sustain you whilst you build your coaching and consulting practice.

Decide on how much you need to live on, what you're prepared to cut in order to go into 'survival' mode and how long you're prepared to do that for. Remember, it takes twice as long to build a business and costs twice as much as you think it will.

I cut my outgoings right down to £1,800 per month when I started. I could pay half the household bills, mortgage and for my car, but not much else. I decided the sacrifice was worth it. You might think differently. It's your choice.

For me, freedom is much more important than earning huge sums of money. It still is. I have invested a huge amount of my consulting and coaching fees into building Tricres. I have taken a cut in my standard of car, clothing and treats to build something bigger. Not everyone wants to do that. Will it pay off? I have no idea. There are no guarantees.

What I can tell you though is I enjoy building Tricres and seeing people like you develop into brilliant coaches and consultants much more than driving a flash car or buying designer shoes. I've still enjoyed a very nice lifestyle, paid half the household bills and live in a beautiful part of the UK.

For me, it's been worth it. You might think differently. You might be lucky enough or well-connected enough to get started with a diary full of high-paying clients and never need to cost cut.

My point here is to decide what you want, then decide what you're prepared to sacrifice to get it. Only you can make that decision. I'd advise talking it over with your nearest and dearest to make sure they're on board!

Here are the practical things you need to consider when setting up your consulting and coaching enterprise.

Will you be a sole trader or a limited company? If you're in the USA, it's likely you'll register as an LLC. If you never intend to employ anyone or increase the size of your business beyond you, it's best to keep it small scale. There's no need to register a company unless the laws of the land state that you have to.

Get yourself a business bank account. In the UK, there are so many options for small businesses, including Starling, Revolut and Tide. Choose a bank that understands small businesses and find one that offers the lowest charges for transactions, etc.

If you're in the UK, it takes about 10 minutes and currently 12 pounds to register a limited company. With your passport and limited company details, you can open a business bank account in around 24 hours. It's never been easier to get started. This might not be the case in other countries, I guess we're lucky here in the UK.

Find a good bookkeeper. Many coaches and consultants are tempted to do their own bookkeeping. Please don't. Even if you've been a bookkeeper or accountant in a previous life, it's better to get someone else to do this. This is because you'll end up getting knee-deep in taxation legislation and tax returns when you should be developing business and servicing clients.

The easiest way to remind yourself of this is to work out what you're worth an hour and then compare that with what you pay a bookkeeper per hour. You can earn much more using your consulting and coaching talents than you can doing spreadsheets.

Use an online accounting tool such as Xero or Quickbooks. These link to your bank account in most cases and will reduce the cost of your bookkeeping fees.

Have a good accountant who can do your annual accounting and tax returns. The business consulting and coaching model is simple. You'll need to check in with your accountant or bookkeeper every quarter to keep on top of cash flow and bills. If things get more complicated than you and a freelancer or two, then you'll need more regular interactions.

Never spend more than you earn. This sounds simple. If you are sticking with a simple coaching and consulting business, then you should never need to spend more than you bring in. If you're going to expand and take other people on, then this might change. That's a whole other book.

Rebecca has left many accountants over the years. She insists she gets proactive advice and support from her suppliers. Never stick with someone who isn't providing you with the service you need. Keep asking around for referrals for accountants and lawyers until you find people you're happy with.

Lawyers. You'll need a lawyer for any terms and conditions you want to issue and for shareholder and director agreements if you're going into business with anyone else. Again, find lawyers who understand small businesses and who charge appropriately. There's no point in going to a multinational law firm and paying thousands of pounds or dollars if it's just you and your cat.

Save money for your tax bills. All governments like to tax you on anything you earn and any profits you make. This varies from country to country so make sure you're up to date with tax thresholds for personal and corporate tax. If you have a good bookkeeper or accountant, they'll tell you what the current rates and allowances are.

The biggest mistake Rebecca made in her first business was not saving to pay a corporate tax bill. It was her first business and she hadn't realised taking dividends meant saving money on personal tax, but also meant tax would be charged on the profits declared by the business. When you bring in 3,000 a month in client fees, make sure you save the correct proportion of that for tax.

In the UK, we save around one-quarter of any dividends we draw and put it in a high-interest account ready for when the government demand their share.

You also need to leave enough cash in the business for a rainy day. Things happen. The unexpected will happen when you least expect it – obvious, but needs pointing out. A good rule of thumb is to have about three month's money sitting in your business bank account at any one time. This might take a while to build up but is worth building for peace of mind.

Again, don't do what Rebecca did when she ran her recruitment business and splash out on a flash car without thinking about the cash that was needed to run the business. We live and learn.

Naming your business. We'll come to that in the next chapter as it relates to your niche and how you brand your business.

Getting a website. This is something else we're leaving for the next chapter as it's tied in with your niche too.

We've given you a QR code (Figure 1.1). This links to one of our online programmes 'Setting You Up To Succeed' which is part of our Business Coach and Consultant Accelerator. Much of the information is directed towards our Tricres coaches, but the principles will apply to you and your business. Please use them.

There are useful videos, downloadable PDFs and a whole course called Double Your Day Rate, which we hope you'll find useful as you grow your business coaching and consulting practice.

Figure 1.1 Setting You Up to Succeed QR Code.

Chapter 2

Finding Your Niche

Step One: Who Are You?

Your business coaching and consulting business is about you. Whilst you might use the Tricres brand and materials or your own or even a franchise business name, your clients are still buying from you. They want you in their business and will recommend you personally.

Much of what is contained in this chapter has been learned from our brand guru, Lauren Jones, please look her up at www.brandbyboudica.com she's awesome.

Leading with your personality therefore makes sense. It's so important to be yourself. Nick and Rebecca have made a career out of being opinionated Mancunians (people from Manchester). They are no-nonsense, straight talking and very direct. Not everyone likes them. That's ok. Not everyone will like you and that's ok too. If everyone likes you, you become bland, boring and uninspiring. As a business coach and consultant that's the last thing you want to be.

The only way to succeed and rise above the noise is to be yourself.

Here's the framework you can use to start describing who you are and what you're about.

Answer the questions below for yourself:

- How would your best friend describe you?
- What are the three coolest things about you? If, you were to be more memorable, are these things you'd like people to know about you?
- How do you weave that into your story/chat? If you haven't yet done that, write it out now.
- Think about the character traits of people you admire.
- Create a list of adjectives that describe you, keep adding to it. Use a Thesaurus to help.
- REMEMBER – you've been able to identify the characteristics/traits of people you admire because they resonate with you and reflect your personality. That is, you already have them within you!

DOI: 10.4324/9781003602422-2

- These are the traits that drive you and the description we invite you to use when introducing yourself, e.g., what type of coach/consultant are you?

If you describe yourself as optimistic, joyful, always bringing lightness and warmth to difficult situations and the stresses of running the business then that's how you should describe yourself when you meet people in networking situations or as a way to introduce yourself.

Step Two: Who Do You Serve?

The following questions are important, so please take your time in answering them truthfully.

- What are your areas of expertise and experience? Are they things you enjoy? Please only write down the areas you enjoy. There is no point in setting up a business coaching and consulting business to escape the 9–5 just to return to work you don't like doing.
- What are the top three clients you've ever had? Or, if you've been in employment, what were the top three roles you had or projects you were involved with?
  - What did you enjoy specifically about these?
  - What kind of people were you working with?
  - What was the topic you were helping people with?
  - Were you working in a particular sector that you found enjoyable?

When you've answered these questions, think about why you enjoyed the elements you enjoyed and the people you enjoyed working with.

Step Three: What Do You Do for Your Clients?

The following questions are also important, so please take your time in answering them truthfully.

- What do you give your clients or allow them to do? If you've been employed, think about the people you've worked alongside or been leading and managing.
- What problem do you solve for your clients, colleagues, etc., that only can solve.

Step Four: How You Show Up

Yes, there's more writing to do. This is about how you back up the claims you're making, so focus!

Finish the following sentence:

"Life and work is more.................................when you work with me".

What are the reasons to believe in you as a business coach and consultant?

1. ....
2. ....
3. ....

For example, wisdom, experience, expertise, case studies, testimonials, sense of humour, fan base, tattoos, life experience, etc.

Think about your style, your approach, the way you talk and present yourself to the world. You might need to ask a friend or trusted business associate the following question, "what's unique about my approach to work?"

Other unique aspects of you might be

- The type of clothing you wear
- Your funky glasses
- Do you have a distinctive voice
- Some people wear red shoes, bright socks, etc. Rebecca gets her nails painted bright colours
- Do you have a 'look' that encompasses a sharp suit, nose ring, tattoos, short hair, long hair, etc.
- Body language. Some people use their arms a lot when they communicate, some stand stock still

Whatever your distinctive style is, it's unique to you. Whatever is on the outside, must match the inside.

Are you the type of business coach who brings a sense of humour to situations? Do you see the big picture when everyone else is down in the detail? Nick wears bright shirts and fancy shoes, he's known for his loud, Mancunian voice too. Rebecca is renowned for asking questions no one else is prepared to ask and for her direct approach.

Who are you and what are you known for?

Think about this and then present it to the world. It's worth reiterating that not everyone will like you. That's ok. It means you're on the right track. Plenty of people will like you and engage with you because you are you.

Step Five: Aligning with Your Brand

If you're a Tricres Coach, this is easy because you've come through our process and already know you're bold, impactful and direct. These are our values and all our materials are designed to portray this. The way we attract new coaches to use our methodology is to describe it as Kick A** and not everyone is going to like that. In fact, we find, the people who love it are precisely the people who identify with our models, frameworks and way of working.

When you think about who you are and how you want to show up in the world, your brand, name and content need to reflect that.

When we started Tricres and our own individual consulting, training and coaching business before that, we both found brand experts who took time to understand who we were and what we stood for. This is a lengthy process and is worth investing time and money into. It's the visible representation of you, so invest wisely. Be smart and invest in a brand that looks bigger than just you. Have someone design a brand, look, imagery and tone of voice that will represent you in ten years.

This sounds silly right now before you have clients, but take our word for it, this content and how you show up to the world will be the difference between charging 500 pounds or dollars a day and 5,000 pounds or dollars a day. The look and feel of your coaching and consulting business will open doors or close them.

This is why so many coaches and consultants join Tricres. We've built the brand, content, imagery and tone of voice so you don't have to. It cost us tens of thousands of pounds.

Finally, be consistent. Whatever you decide your brand look, feel and tone of voice will be, you need to be consistent about it. Whatever platform you gain business from or whether you stick with more traditional face-to-face networking, everything you hand out, talk about and share must be consistent with your brand.

We are not branding experts, but we've given you access to Lauren Jones' superb course "Building A Brilliant Brand" which will give you a headstart. Just scan the QR code in Figure 2.1. It's a great course to do BEFORE you see a brand consultant, you can hand them the documents Lauren shows you how to complete and save yourself a small fortune in fees!

This section is about putting your head above the parapet. Nick goes into a lot of detail on networking and following up after networking, so this section is more about shifting your mindset and giving yourself a huge kick up the backside to get out there.

You may have the best experience, the best knowledge and the best approach to business coaching and consulting in the world, but if you don't tell anyone about it, no one will ever know.

If you are feeling shy about 'exposing' yourself to ridicule, and negative comments online or simply feel underconfident about showcasing what you do, then this section will give you some exercises to overcome those feelings.

Figure 2.1 Building a Brilliant Brand QR Code.

I'm going to let you into a secret. For decades, I didn't think I was experienced or clever enough to be a business coach. I sincerely believed that was for special people with special skills and a special background. I had gone to a state school, got a very mediocre degree, failed to secure a graduate job after finishing university and had fallen off the corporate ladder at the age of 27. I've never grown and exited a business for millions or even thousands, I've never held a CEO role in a company that wasn't my own and I don't have any friends in high places.

All in all, I felt extremely underqualified to consider myself as a business coach. I'm now going to show you how to get over those feelings.

First of all, write out a list of all the negative beliefs you have about yourself. It might be similar to the one I just wrote, or it could be different. Get them all out on paper. Every single one of them.

Then, take that piece of paper and go outside and set fire to it. Yes, I literally want you to set fire to all those unhelpful beliefs about yourself. Do it safely. If you can't set fire to it, then shred it in a shredding machine. Destroy it somehow so you can never read it again.

Once you've done that, I'd like you to grab a coffee, tea or glass of water and write out all the reasons why you'd make a brilliant business coach and consultant.

This is what I focused on.

I'd been in the recruitment industry for 15 years. Many people look down on this industry and belittle it. However, I realised I'd interviewed on average, two people a day for 15 years who were either finance directors, lawyers, or partners in professional services and I'd visited hundreds of different types of businesses all at different stages of growth.

It dawned on me that this had been the best research into businesses, business models and the behaviours of business people anyone could have had. Instead of beating myself up about wasting time as a recruiter, I decided to celebrate the 15 years of solid research I'd conducted into growing businesses.

Next, I had to deal with the niggling belief that other people would be pointing their fingers at me and saying things like 'who does she think she is, she can't be a business coach'.

To tackle this, I went to see a few business coaches do presentations, and talks followed their content online and generally got a bit nosey. Some of them were fantastic and I learned a lot from them. Most of them were average and one or two were terrible. Even the terrible ones were getting clients and clients who thought they were amazing.

This made me realise, just like relationships, there's someone out there for everyone. It doesn't matter what kind of human being you are or what kind of experience you have, there will be a business owner out there who adores you and thinks you're perfect for what they need right now. There are almost nine billion people on the planet and millions of businesses, this means you have a 100% chance to align with at least three or four businesses in the world each month and make a decent living from coaching and consulting.

Now we've dealt with the fears that are holding you back, (if you want more on this, then please check out the QR code at the end of this section as it takes you to our Thinking Big (Really Big) programme (Figure 2.2). It contains everything you need to re-design your self-image) let's get on with how you get out there.

There are many ways and here are just a few ideas:

1. Social media, pick one platform and build your audience on it. Once you've built your audience on one platform you can start on another and then another, until you have the major platforms covered. At this stage, I'd highly recommend using a scheduling tool such as Painless Posting (here's a link https://painlessposting.com/plp-optin?am_id=rebecca3199). Eventually, you can use a freelance assistant to do this for you.

   If you're sitting there wondering about ideas for content, then here's someone else we recommend, Ashley Leeds' book *101 Ideas For LinkedIn, Content Made Easy* (https://www.amazon.co.uk/stores/author/B0BJLD2KLV)

   Finally, if you're a Tricres coach then we give you lots of content you can use to post on your socials and a LinkedIn 101 course to get you into some good habits. Our main platform is LinkedIn, yours might be different. Please get support and guidance from people who know what they're doing on the platform your audience is on.

   In today's world, it's very difficult to get out there without being on social media. If you think that having a website is enough, then you're going to be very disappointed. We've learned the hard way that driving traffic to your website is difficult. You need to understand SEO (search engine optimisation) and keywords to stand a chance of being 'found'. By all means, have a website that you can direct people to when you're posting on social media, but don't think having a website will mean people will type in 'business coach' and find you. They won't.

In recent months, we've found having an up-to-date Google Business Page is as important as posting on LinkedIn. We use Painless Posting to schedule posts on our Google Business Page and treat it just like any other social media content. It helps you move up the Google searches, but it doesn't put you at number one!

Things change constantly on social media, so please research the best place for your content and the latest trends.

2. Events and networking. In the early days of building your business coaching business, go to everything. Try out your local business networking groups and find the ones that suit you and your target audience. In the UK, we have the Institute of Directors and across the UK and the USA there's BNI and Chambers of Commerce. Use Event Bright to search for business events in your area too.

   Once you're at the networking events start asking around about the best ones to go to and sign up with. Almost all networking groups will give you at least one try before you buy a session, giving you the opportunity to work out if it's right for you.

   Online networking blossomed during COVID-19 and until that point was possibly seen as a poor relation to face-to-face networking. However, things have changed. There are many very professional networking groups that provide excellent connections for business coaches and consultants.

   We recommend an online networking group called ONLE, use our affiliate link to receive a discount on your membership fee. Here are the details:

   When you sign up, use the discount code *TRICRES to* get a whopping 50% off. Here's the link to join https://theonle.network/

Do not be put off by the number of other coaches in these spaces. There will be many. The good news is, none of them are you. You are unique. Your approach, style, knowledge, experience and skills are completely unique to you. It's you that business owners will engage with.

Yes, there will be highly experienced business coaches in the room who may make you feel inferior or 'not worthy'. Ignore them. They are not you. Often the more experienced coaches are a bit cocky or ego-driven (not always, but often). Use your style and your personality to differentiate yourself from others. Be open, and be willing to give some of your time and expertise for free as a 'taste' of what you're capable of delivering.

Above all, talk about and ask about the people who are in the room and their business. Be curious about them and be genuinely interested. Never 'sell' yourself. There's no need. When you strike up a great conversation and demonstrate your ability to listen, ask great questions and perhaps offer some quick tips or ideas for the people you're talking with, business owners will love you.

They will be drawn to you and not the person who is spending ten minutes rambling on about how great they are and how all their clients adore them. Yawn. No one likes a show-off and no one wants to work with arrogant people who are driven by their own egos.

I feel very passionately about this. I've seen far too many business coaches think they're God's gift to business. Let's get one thing straight, when you're a business coach and consultant your role is to facilitate the success of the client and they own their outcomes. You are the sounding board, the wise head, the person who asks difficult questions and the person who listens carefully, sharing thoughts and ideas to be tested by the business. You are not the person who does all the work on the ground.

I've found winning clients to be a simple process of showing up consistently at the same networking groups, having really good conversations with people and following up with further conversations later. This doesn't always lead to paid work, but it leads to some paid work and a great deal of goodwill from people who are happy to recommend you to others.

Network your socks off in the first couple of years, build your base through a humble, interested approach and remember it's not about you, it's about your clients and their needs.

Getting out there also includes giving talks. In the very early stages of my coaching business, I gave free talks to the Chamber of Commerce in Edinburgh, The Institute of Directors, The Entrepreneurial Exchange and quite a few others I've forgotten about.

These talks gave me three things: an audience I could follow up with, practice working with my materials and refining them and confidence. I said 'yes' to every offer to speak, no matter how small the audience was (sometimes it was two people!). It got my name out there and connected me with some great people.

I ended up speaking at the opening of an international conference in London at the headquarters of a global bank! All this gave my potential clients the 'social proof' they needed to have confidence in using me. They didn't need to know I wasn't being paid and they certainly didn't need to know that on one occasion it was an audience of two people.

This led to large amounts of work with people who I still occasionally work with today. I was very happy to give my time for free to membership organisations and to not-for-profits, but I stopped doing the 'lunch and learn' freebies for corporates and larger SMEs. I delivered one such lunch and learned to a very large public sector organisation who promised work on the back of my 'free sample'. This never materialised. When the head of learning and development of a very large law firm asked me to do a free lunch and learn with their partners I said 'no'.

A large firm has very deep pockets, and so do large public sector organisations. It was at that point I vowed only to give my time for free when everyone else was giving their time for free. The final straw was an insurance company that invited me to speak at the conference for free. I duly did and sat next to a guy who was also delivering a talk that day. He was getting paid and I wasn't. From then on, I always check to see who is getting paid and who isn't and what type of event it is.

By all means, give your time for free to gain audiences and leads, but do it with caution and don't be the only person giving your time away for free at the event!

When I started, we didn't have the podcast culture we do now. This is the other way of getting yourself seen and heard.

You can either be a guest on other people's podcasts or start your own. The details of setting up your podcast or marketing yourself to be invited on as a guest onto other people's podcasts would fill an entire book.

Writing a book is another way of 'getting out there'. Again, that would take up another book.

Suffice it to say, the easier wins are telling everyone you meet what you do, networking, speaking and social media. Once you've got confident with those, you can think about books and podcasts!

Some of you will might have read my book *Building Businesses from the Inside Out* or maybe familiar with our online Kick A** Culture Coach and Consulting programme, some of you may not.

Either way, the next part is about focusing on you and your business. You may have seen or used the Tricres Economic Engine with clients or simply read about it in my previous book, but I'm curious to know whether you've applied it to your own business coaching and consulting business. If you've never seen it before, don't panic, I'm going to walk you through each step so you can apply the principles to your own business.

Figure 2.2 Thinking Big (Really Big) QR Code.

The Tricres Economic Engine Model

First of all, I'm hoping you've gathered by now that you are running your own business. Whilst it may only be you and may only ever be you, it's still a business and needs to be treated in the same way as a larger entity.

The mistake I made at the start of my own coaching and consulting business enterprise was that I got a logo done, and a website set up and then didn't think about anything beyond that except getting paying clients. There were several steps missing and I learned the hard way that you can't miss any of the steps out. I don't want you to make the same mistakes I did.

Figure 2.3 is an image of the Tricres Economic Engine Model.

Let's go through each of the circles in turn, please make notes and relate them back to your own business.

Circle One: Purpose

For what purpose does your business coaching and consulting business exist beyond profit? This is the Simon Sinek 'Why'. If you haven't yet seen his

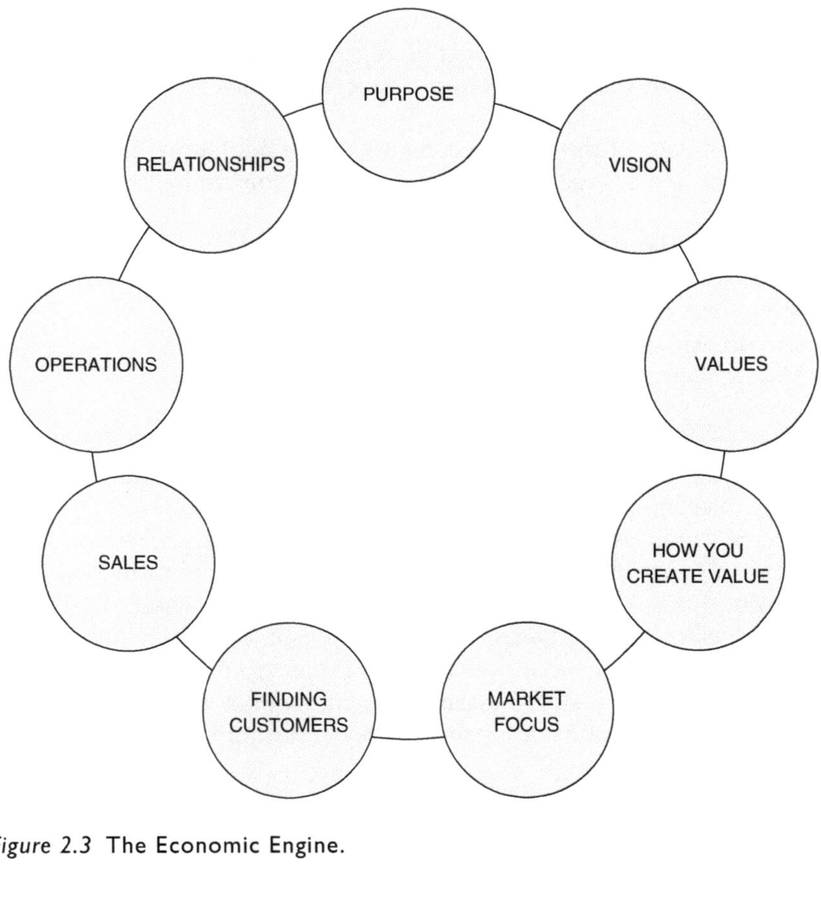

Figure 2.3 The Economic Engine.

2009 TEDTalk called "How Great Leaders Inspire Action", then I advise you to watch it.

These are the questions you need to ask yourself:

- What do I give my clients or allow them to do?
- What's the ultimate reason for the existence of my business?

Your purpose is eternal. It doesn't change. It's the guiding light that you follow no matter what. When I was out on my own, my purpose was to 'think differently and achieve more'. It was entirely focused on leadership development and my foundations were grounded in NLP. As my business developed, it became clear that this was no longer my purpose. I realised that simply working with leaders wasn't enough, and I had to go back to the drawing board to find out what I wanted and what my purpose was.

I spent two years not knowing which direction to go in. Apart from driving my husband mad with the number of changes I made, I didn't want to pin my colours to any particular mast until it really resonated with me. The process started with trying things out and realised what I absolutely didn't want and ultimately led to a four-day retreat in the Highlands doing collages with a bunch of tree huggers. It was an experience that pushed me right out of my comfort zone and that's where I found my next purpose.

So, don't panic if this doesn't come to you straight away. Explore, test, reject, refine and change tack until you settle on something that feels right to you.

Here are some other examples I've come across:

- Bring form to clients' values – architects' firm
- Can do, will do, have done – construction company
- Make it happen – Tricres

You can see the phrases are very high level, there is no detail and they inspire an emotional response. This is the kind of thing you're after. Your purpose is unlikely to change even if your coaching business needs to pivot.

Tricres began as a training app for business owners. Training other coaches and consultants was a side project. It became obvious that business owners didn't want to learn about coaching and consulting in their own businesses, they still wanted a real person to help them with that so we changed direction and moved our side project to the forefront of what we do. Our purpose is still to make it happen, we're now making it happen for business coaches and consultants so they in turn can make it happen for their clients.

Some top tips to help you find your purpose:

- Think about where you bring the most value
- Think about what gives you energy and brings you joy
- Create a vision board of you working with your ideal clients in an ideal way
- Search out words and phrases that make your heart sing
- Be patient, it will come

Once you've found a series of words that feel right, write them up where you can see them. Read them every day, say them out loud and tell people what your purpose is. Use the purpose statement in your proposals, documents and marketing materials. Share it with whoever is designing your brand. It will help position you in the market place and stand out from the crowd.

Circle Two: Vision

This is about where you want your business to be in ten years. A ten-year timescale is far enough into the future that you need to imagine what it will be like. You have to guess. Yes, you will be making it up. If you're going to make something up, you may as well make it good.

Think about where you'd like your business coaching and consulting business to be ten years from now. Write down the date and year which will be exactly ten years from now. Then start getting creative. If you struggle with this, Tricres has an entire programme called Thinking Big (Really Big) online, the QR Code for this was at the end of the last section (Figure 2.2).

If you're having fun with this idea already, then really go for it. Think about the types of clients you want to be working with ten years from now, how much they'll be paying you, where you'll be working geographically and what type of work you'll be doing.

Make it big, bold, fun and exciting. This is the vision that will keep you going through the tough times. It's the vision that will get you up in the morning, excited about going to another networking event or travelling 200 miles to give a talk. You must make it emotionally compelling so you keep going.

Use magazines, pens, pencils and colours to draw out your vision. Find keywords that excite your imagination and add those to the images you've created. My vision included my family and friends as well as my clients and my work. It's so important you include good health, well-being and joy into your vision. This is your business and your vision, craft something that is unique to you. It doesn't matter that right at this moment in time you have no idea how you're going to achieve any of it. That will come later.

Here's an insight into my vision. This vision was created before I started Tricres. It consisted of me standing at the top of a castle which was at the top of a hill, overlooking the sea. There were lots of people in the picture that I was supporting and nurturing (I had depicted myself as a queen!). This hand-drawn image (badly drawn, I might add) was then translated into a collage with images of boats, yachts, beautiful homes in Italy, family, friends and healthy living. It included a cosy room with a yellow sofa and a log-burning stove too. I mention this because last year my husband built me a garden room which has a yellow sofa and a log-burning stove. I only realised the room matched my vision about six months after he'd finished!

The yachts and homes in Italy haven't appeared yet. I know they will though. I don't know in what form, but they will appear in my life.

The people overseas have appeared too. These are the people like you that we're training to be business coaches and consultants. I and my team are nurturing and supporting them to succeed and enjoy the kind of life they've always dreamed of.

This is a fun exercise.

The vision that came out for the business was as follows:

To be the most successful business consulting and coaching business in the world. Success is defined as seeing someone on the side of a hill in Nepal using our content to help their business grow.

Interestingly this did not change when we shifted our focus from business owners to business coaches and consultants. Your vision is unlikely to shift too much even as your business changes. I would add that if you run this exercise properly, and fully engage with the fun, free spirit of it, then your vision will remain steadfast no matter how much your business model changes. That's because the vision comes from your heart, not your head. If your vision feels right to you and you have a strong, personal, emotional connection to it, then it's right.

You'll notice too that the vision doesn't contain numbers, facts, dates or deadlines. It's ten years from now, you can't possibly include those. Keep the images you create, refer to them once a year and notice what you've already achieved. It will never look exactly like the images you've created, but you'll have a version of it that's right for you. Without getting too spiritual about it, the universe/life/your chosen deity delivers what you need, not what you think you want.

Once you've been able to write your vision out in a few words, phrases or sentences, pin it up where you can see it and look at it every day. Memorise it and use it when you're talking to people. It's something you can share with your clients if you wish and include in your marketing materials. It helps your prospective clients understand whether you're right for them.

Circle Three: Values

Because your coaching and consulting business is likely to be you and you alone, the values you have for your business are going to be closely aligned with your personal values.

At Tricres we believe in the power of three. Pick three values because any more becomes difficult to remember. There are some simple questions you can answer which will help you define the values of your business, these are:

- What's great about working in your business?
- What are you brilliant at?
- What would your competitors be envious of?
- If your business had a personality or character, how would you describe it?

These questions will have more than one-word answers but as full and honest as you can be when answering them. Once you've answered these questions, you'll begin to see a pattern emerging. Some words or phrases will be repeated, make sure you highlight these.

Some words and phrases will resonate with you more than others, again highlight these. Some of the words and phrases you've written down won't feel quite right, but they'll trigger other words and phrases in your mind that do feel right, write those down too.

Now, step back. Literally, take a step away from your desk or table and do something else. Make a cup of tea, pop to the bathroom or stare out of the window. You need to break your state and come back to the words and phrases with a fresh pair of eyes.

Ok, now look at the words and phrases.

What stands out?

Whittle the words and phrases down to three. Don't worry, you can keep everything you've written down as the additional words and phrases are likely to appear in the meanings of the values and the behaviours you'll be writing down.

Figure 2.4 is an example of the values grid you're going to create for your own coaching and consulting business.

At this point, you might be thinking this is overkill. You're a one-person band with no intention of having employees or growing beyond yourself. Let me reassure you, this little grid will stop you from spending money on things you don't need, it will stop you from engaging with the wrong clients, it will help you make decisions faster and save your time and money and most importantly, it will give you an experience of the kinds of things you're going to be asking your clients to do.

VALUE	MEANING	BEHAVIOUR	SUPPORTING SYSTEM
Bold	• Brave • Fearless • Challenging	• We stand by what we say • We say it as it is • We are leaders	• Our branding and marketing • Our growth plans • International expansion
Impactful	• Disruptive • Inspiring • Empowering	• We challenge the status quo • We instill belief • We make it happen, quicker	• Our learning platform • Our coaching, consulting and training methodology • Our lack of bureaucracy
Direct	• Agile • Creative • Game-changing	• We are flexible • We think outside the box • We deliver WOW results	• Each partner learns a new skill every year • We welcome feedback in all of its forms • We are avid readers, consumers of relevant expertise in all its formats

Figure 2.4 Values Grid, Completed.

Many clients, coaches and consultants are impressed that I and Tricres practice what we preach. It doesn't impress me, I take it as a given that we follow the methods we show our clients and coaches how to use. If I'm not prepared to use them myself or in my business, then I have no right to ask my clients or coaches to do the same. Using the methods we train people in means we can give real-life insights into how they work and tweak them when they don't work. The same applies to you and your business.

Please share your value with your prospects and your clients. It helps them make a decision as to whether you're the right person for them. Make the values unique to you. If you've got integrity in there, take it out, that's a given. Be bold, be you. Your personality and style need to shine through these values, meanings and behaviours. They form the language you'll use when speaking to people at networking events. They'll help you form great proposals, shape the tone of voice of your business and win you work.

My advice to you is to spend time on the purpose, vision and values of your business. Test them out, and make decisions that are aligned with your values to check they're right for you. This will mean turning down clients and potentially lucrative work if it doesn't align with your values. Rest assured though, if you accept work that doesn't align with your values, at the very least it will make you miserable and at the worst, it will cost you money. I speak from bitter experience! I've walked away from very lucrative retainers because the business owner was nasty and treated their team appallingly. Whilst my decision negatively impacted my bank balance in the short term, in the medium term it created space for the right kind of clients. This in turn led to longer term and much more lucrative working relationships.

If any of you have recently left the corporate world, I'm guessing one of the key reasons is that the business did not align with your core values and it was making you ill. Remember that for your own business.

Circle Four: How You Create Value

This circle is about the focus of your business. Is it a service-driven business or a product-driven business?

There's a very quick and easy way to define this.

If you know the names of your client's children, pets and partners and know where they go on holiday, you're running a service-driven business. The sales cycle for this type of business (sales cycle is from the time you first connect with a prospective client to the time you invoice them) tends to be about three months to two years. If you win clients within three months of setting up, then you're doing really well. Most self-employed business coaches and consultants are running a service-driven business.

If you don't know the names of your client's children, pets or partners and you've no idea where they go on holiday, then you're likely to be running a product-driven business. Product-driven businesses tend to run on a shorter sales cycle. This can be anything from an hour to a week or two, perhaps stretching out to a month or two at most.

At Tricres we initially began as a service-driven business. My brother and I delivered our services one-to-one to clients and we knew them extremely well, some of them became friends. We built the online learning platform to transition to a product-driven business. We naively thought this would build very quickly and we'd be super wealthy within a year or two and be able to retire to a beach somewhere. This didn't happen because we were utterly clueless about how incredibly difficult it is to build sales for online learning platforms (that's a whole other book!).

So, unless you want a whole world of heartache, pain and cost, stick with the service-driven model for your coaching and consulting business. If you want to talk to us about the product-driven model, then we're happy to give you the whole story, warts and all!

Having a service-driven business does not mean you can't have products. In fact, later in this book, I talk you through how to develop products to help improve your sales. However, at the very heart of your business is the service-led approach. You get to know your clients very well, you deliver a bespoke service to them, albeit with some consistent models and frameworks that can be packaged up as 'products' and you keep in touch regularly, send them gifts, take them out for lunch and meet with them even when they're not buying anything.

Your clients are a long-term relationship in a service-driven business. You must speak to them at least once a year because when they need you, they'll come back to you and not another coach and consultant who is already hammering on their door. Nurture these relationships, give value, share ideas, connections, articles, thoughts and insights and cherish them. If you ignore these people, you will not get repeat business or referrals.

These are the people who will recommend you, even when you don't ask to be recommended. They will remember you years later and refer people to you. I had someone refer their colleague to me last week, I hadn't worked with this client for over five years, but I'd kept track of her every job move and promotion on LinkedIn, diligently sending her a personal message each time she moved. She didn't reply to any of my messages until last week. She was reading them though and noting that I was keeping in touch.

I cannot stress to you enough how vital it is you keep an eye on your previous clients, near-miss clients and those people you meet at events, etc. Use LinkedIn to notice their birthdays, job moves, life events and comments. Phone when it's something really important, meet for coffee every now and again. I promise it will lead to business, perhaps not immediately or even in a few months, but it will lead to business.

You're a service-driven business. Be of service at all times.

Circle Five: Market Focus

This circle relates to the part of Nick's sales process called 'Target'. He goes into a huge amount of detail on that so I'm keeping it brief here.

Have a focus. Keep it sharp, follow the money and stay on track. In the early days of your business coaching and consulting business, it's important to remain as focused on a single market sector as you possibly can.

Many of you will have a concern over being 'too focused' and missing out on other opportunities. I promise you this won't happen. What does happen is that you become known for a particular specialism or in a particular market. Then, other people outside of that specialism or market start asking you if you can help them.

Select a market where you can do your best work, where you enjoy working with those kinds of people and where you can earn good money.

The easiest way to identify the best market for you is to answer the following questions:

- Who do I love working with? What kind of people or businesses do I really enjoy working with?
- What kind of projects do I love working on and what does that work involve?
- Where have I had the most success over the past few years?

Once you've answered those questions, you'll very quickly identify which market is right for you. Even if you've been working in a salaried position for the past few years, there will be clients or colleagues that you've enjoyed working with more than others. There will be aspects of the business you enjoyed more than others and there will have been projects, secondments, etc., that particularly stood out for you.

If you're going to go out on your own, you may as well do the work you love with the people you love working with. Otherwise, stay in a job.

Finally, saying 'no' to clients is the most powerful thing you can do. I did it last week. There was a chap who wanted to join our Kick Ass Culture Coach and Consultant Training programme, he had a few questions and doubts so I called him. After speaking to him it was crystal clear the programme wasn't right for him and he wasn't a good fit culturally. I simply let him know he shouldn't spend his money with us as it wasn't right for him.

It's tempting to say 'yes' to all clients, particularly when you're starting out. My advice is to say 'yes' at first so you can work out what kind of clients you definitely don't want to work with. Then, as you work out your ideal client, only say 'yes' to them. My rule is simple, if I like you, I'll work with you. You've got to meet me halfway and put in the effort, otherwise I will let you go as a client.

This system keeps me sane, allows me to continue to love the work I do and saves me a huge amount of pain, time and wasted energy. When I look back, the best clients were the ones who never questioned any of my invoices or value. The ones I should not have taken on always questioned my invoice and my value. Lesson learned!

Circle Six: Finding Customers

Now you know who your target market is, you need to go and find them. I describe this as 'hanging out where your clients hang out'.

If your clients are on Instagram, you need to be on there. If they're on LinkedIn, then that's where you need to be. Some of you will be asking, 'How do I know where my customers hang out?'

The answer is easy: find your nearest similar competitor and see where they hang out. I follow Daniel Priestly obsessively. He's been building businesses for decades and is a multi-millionaire. I cannot compete with him (we do different things anyway), but a lot of his clients are business coaches and consultants so I hang out where he hangs out, which is LinkedIn and X.

In the early days, you might need to test a few platforms to be sure. A good rule of thumb is that if your clients are business owners, they're on LinkedIn. If they are involved in fashion, the arts, creative industries, hospitality, fashion, retail, beauty, travel, etc., then they're more than likely going to be on Instagram. If your target market is over 45 and loves family things, then it's likely they're on Facebook. If your target market is under 25, they're on TikTok. You get the idea.

YouTube is great, but appears to be male-dominated so if you're a female-focused coach, it's probably not the right platform for you.

This is finding customers online. You need to post regularly, share value, give people free information and interact in a very human way. If you turn up once a week on any of the platforms, you won't be seen. You have to be there at least three or four times a week and you must comment, respond to messages and be yourself. You cannot be political unless that's your business proposition as you may end up getting blocked or banned. Speak to people in these spaces as though you were speaking to them in real life.

As your revenues grow, I advise you to use a social media scheduling tool such as Painless Posting, here's the link https://painlessposting.com/plp-optin?am_id=rebecca3199 so you can spend a few hours each week scheduling your posts for the following couple of weeks. This will save you a huge amount of time and energy.

When you are even more successful, I suggest getting the help of a virtual assistant to do your posting for you.

Finding your clients in the real world. You have to turn up in real life too. We've talked a lot about networking and finding the right kind of networking events for you. Use a combination of local and international networks, both online and in person. Turn up to everything and then whittle it down to two or three that you show up to consistently. Be the helpful person in the room and for goodness sake remember to follow up with coffees, Zoom calls and meetings.

It took me four years to land a global bank as a client. The average time it takes me to win a business coaching and consulting client is six months. You need to be patient, consistent and always follow up. Last week I had a coffee with a business owner with whom I'd worked with for four years. I knew they weren't in a position to use me at the moment, but I wanted to keep in touch. Three days later they asked me to help them with something. It's always worth keeping in touch, especially when your clients aren't actively buying from you.

Conferences, exhibitions, talks, opening events, awards ceremonies, etc., all are events you need to go to. If your sector has a membership organisation, find out about joining and attend their annual conference. If you have the money, become a sponsor of their events. Offer to speak at their local meetings and events for free. Get yourself known in those circles. Connect with other suppliers in that market. I've had two fantastic referrals from another coach who does something very differently to me and won two great clients. We met at an online group for suppliers to law firms.

Circle Seven: Sales

Again, Nick covers this in his four-step process; Target, Connect, Meet Ask. If you're in any doubt, what he shows you is a sales process. If you've done the first six circles and you know who you're talking to, how you're saying it, where to find them and then follow his four steps, you will get clients.

I'm going to say it again and do so unapologetically; consistency is key. It's not a very exciting or inspiring message, some parts of running your business coaching and consulting business will be repetitive, but it's the single most important message I can give you at this point in the book.

Following the process once will get you nowhere. Following it, a thousand times for years will give you a great business coaching practice with plenty of great clients.

Circle Eight: Operations

Almost all business coaches and consultants are one-man or one-woman bands. This means you don't have to spend too much time thinking about operations. The business model for consulting and coaching is a very simple one: you ask great questions, listen and then match your offering to answer those questions (if appropriate). Then you meet the client, do the work and send an invoice. There's not a huge amount of operational complexity involved.

However, there are some very simple things you can follow which will smooth this journey for you and your clients. I've written this in the form of a list. I suggest you tick off the items on the list you've already got in place, look into the others and consider adding them into your processes.

- Have a simple CRM (customer relationship management system) to record the essential information about your prospects and clients (HubSpot, Pipedrive and Zoho are all good options) with the ability to add reminders to contact and follow up with people
- Have a few templates set up in Word or Pages that you can use when contacting clients either on LinkedIn or via email. Use Nick's suggestions to make them more human
- Have a template set up for an 'update note', these are the updates I send out after each interaction with a client. They keep me and the client and track. They always have a Next Steps section at the end so actions are completed
- Have a template ready for any proposal documents you give or send out
- Set yourself up with a social media content scheduling tool

- Have an electronic diary/calendar booking system. This saves hours going backwards and forwards trying to get dates in the dairy
- Write a To Do list at the end of each day and look at it first thing in the morning
- Book your holidays in your diary a year in advance (not strictly operations, but very important)
- Use your CRM to remind you to keep in touch with clients who aren't buying from you at the moment
- Each business is different, but you may want to have an email contact list that you send useful information to, a newsletter to or simply update with business news relevant to your area of expertise and their businesses

Finally, make sure you have an online accounting system like Xero or Quickbooks and online banking where possible. This makes invoicing and managing your money so much easier.

Circle Nine: Relationships

This is about keeping in touch with people when they're not actively buying from you.

If you're on LinkedIn every day, this is easy. Use the LinkedIn "Catch Up" tab to wish people a happy birthday, acknowledge promotions and job moves and make sure you follow the company pages of your clients. You'll need to comment and share their news to demonstrate you are engaged and interested.

Send Christmas cards, birthday cards, flowers, presents, etc., to those clients with whom you have a fantastic relationship and keep up to date with their personal news (assuming they share it). I have clients who share their news with me via WhatsApp. They always make the first move and I respond at their pace. I am a woman and so I only do this with other women. For me personally, it wouldn't feel right to share more personal updates with a male client. Everyone is different though, so use your judgement.

One of the best ways to keep those relationships going is to hold private dinners. I used to hold this three times a year and joined forces with a law firm and an accounting firm. Each of us invited two clients, booked a private dining room and shared the cost of the food and drink. They were a huge success and we all got clients from it.

I've invited clients to comedy events, quizzes, dinners, lunches, awards, etc., and they always accept. It's an easy and relatively inexpensive way of saying thank you to your clients and keeping up to date with their news.

A quick phone call, an e-card or a handwritten note are extremely effective too. They're also very low cost.

Figure 2.5 Economic Engine QR Code.

You will win most of your work from previous clients, so keep in touch with them at least once or twice a year.

As a self-employed business coach and consultant, you are the income generator for your business. Without you, you don't have a business. This means you need to look after yourself physically, emotionally and spiritually.

Before any of you attempt to start feeling bad about taking time off or nipping out to get your nails done (I do that every four weeks), let me use an analogy.

In a factory, the machinery often works 24 hours a day and 7 days a week. The machinery is the economic engine of the business because without it, nothing would be produced and there would be nothing to sell. You are the machinery of your business.

Every year or on a stricter timetable, the machinery is stopped, cleaned, maintained and adjusted so it can continue to produce what it needs to. The same principle applies to you.

This is the pattern I follow to avoid burning out, you will create your own, but this could be a good starting point:

- Monday and Friday are days I block out from my diary. No one can book calls on these days. I use them to catch up with running my business, administration and downtime. I try to avoid doing client work on a Friday if possible and use Friday to exercise, meet friends and check my emails. Sometimes I do need to do client work on these days, but not often
- Tuesday, Wednesday and Thursday are full on working days. I have availability from 09:30 to 4 pm in my online calendar and will always book client work during these days wherever possible
- At the start of each year, I schedule my holidays. I block off the days I'm taking away from the business and book a holiday. These times tend to coincide with school holidays so I very rarely miss client work

- I take tea and coffee breaks at least twice a day during the day even when I'm working from home and I sit down and eat lunch, even if it's only for 20 minutes. I start work each day at about 9–9:30 am and finish at around 4:30–5:30 pm depending on what I'm delivering or working on
- I switch my phone off at dinner time in the evening and don't check it again until breakfast the next day
- I exercise twice a week, walk my dogs twice a day, get a massage once a month and get my hair and nails done during the week. All of which leaves the weekends free to enjoy with family and friends.

This routine has been going on for about 15 years. I can earn six-figure sums, see clients all over the UK and Ireland, travel overseas for work, write several books and build a new business from scratch.

That's not showing off. It's designed to help you understand that it's not the hours you put in, it's how focused you are during those hours and about switching off regularly so you have more energy to give during your working hours. Writing this book is a brilliant example: I set myself a deadline, allocated time to write and then wrote.

Bob Proctor once said, your results only show up in two places; your calendar and your bank account. He was right. If it's not in my diary, it doesn't happen. I schedule all my events, including family and social events. This means I'm not carrying around a million things in my head and I can't double book myself. To be fair, I have double booked myself on quite a few occasions, but with my electronic booking system, that happens a lot less than it used to!

Scheduling time to look after your mental, physical and spiritual well-being is as important as scheduling time for business development and client work. I meditate twice a day (not every day, but as often as I can) which, alongside my twice daily dog walks, acts as my spiritual nourishment. You may have other practices that fulfil that side of your human needs.

My additional learning, courses I attend and events I go to are also counted as supporting my well-being. Never, ever feel guilty about fulfilling these needs. It's about balance. You work hard to build your business coaching and consulting business so you need to enjoy downtime and relaxation with your friends and family. You have to do a great deal of thinking about your clients and their businesses, so you need mental downtime to recharge the grey cells in your brain. You need to be innovative and think 12 steps ahead of your clients, so you need additional learning from people outside of your area of expertise.

If you're not nourishing your mind, body and soul regularly then you're letting your clients down. It's as simple as that.

If money is tight, then walking in nature is free. If you live in a city, then visit a park, look up at the sky, visit a museum, art gallery or botanical garden. Swim in the local pool, run outside and do online yoga. Read a book from the library. There are so many ways to nurture yourself that don't cost the earth or are completely free. Eat well and sleep well.

What's the point in taking that leap of faith in yourself to become a self-employed business coach and consultant if you can't enjoy time off? You may as well have stayed as an employee.

Chapter 3

How Do You Find Clients Who Want to Work with You?

TARGET and CONNECT (Stages One and Two)

This chapter is written by Nick Davies. He teaches top lawyers this stuff and they pay him handsomely for it, so pay attention.

Before we get into finding clients who want to pay to work with you, allow us to address 'Selling'. Some people are distinctly uncomfortable with it. Or, more accurately, with their perception of it.

Selling

Wherever you are reading this book, stop, put it down and look around. See all that stuff? Everything you see is there because someone sold it! Everything!

The chair you are sitting on, the lights and ceiling panels above you, the desks, the coffee, the sticky bun, the cups, the air conditioning units, the pen you've got, your clothes, shoes, make-up, back-pack, the aircraft, bus, train or car you travelled on to get here – someone, somewhere sold it!

Selling is vital to our society. Organisations only make a profit if they sell something for a price greater than it costs. Out of that profit, they pay corporation tax along with wages to employees who in turn pay tax. No sales = no profit = no tax.

Doctors, nurses, teachers, firefighters, and police officers don't generate profit, which means they have to be paid from tax money. Tax money, which, is only generated if someone, somewhere down the line is selling stuff. We should be happy some people can sell.

Selling – What Is It?

Selling is about making it easy for people to buy. There you are, that's what selling is. 36 years of sales experience and that's the whole lot summed up in ten words.

I suppose you could put the book back on the shelf now and save yourself a few quid?

DOI: 10.4324/9781003602422-3

'Selling' is a dirty word.

At the start of my business development courses, I sometimes ask the delegates to shout out words, phrases and images that come to mind when they hear the word 'sales' or 'salesperson'. Below are the things people say (up and down the country).

- Smooth (but not in a good way),
- Don't listen
- Dishonest
- Pushy
- Second-hand cars
- 'Making you buy something that you don't want'.

Not good is it? And unsurprising, therefore, that some people feel uncomfortable about going out there and promoting their goods or services: with those kinds of feelings associated with sales who would feel comfortable about selling anything?

Once I have allowed them to vent their spleen and disgorge themselves of all this pent-up anger and frustration, I go on to ask if they can recall a time when they were sold and it was a good experience.

Thankfully, most can do this and once again, I hear the same positive characteristics repeated. The good salespeople:

- Listened to me
- Were polite
- Were genuinely interested in what I wanted
- Knew their stuff
- Were able to give advice
- Suggested things that I'd not initially thought of
- Were helpful
- Took time with me

We have all experienced this kind of salesperson and quite likely left their company with less cash but very comfortable with the whole experience and our purchase but, they exemplify something I said earlier – they made it easy for you to buy!

'People buy from people'. Some of you will be familiar with that phrase and it's true. To be more accurate, one should add…'they like' or perhaps, 'that they warm to'.

Why People Buy

You really do need to know why people are buying your product or service. Not just what they want but rather, what they need.

To explain the difference between wants and needs I reckon the hackneyed old 'drill' story is worth trotting out.

Very few people yearn to own a drill (a yacht or villa, perhaps but not a drill) and that includes people walking into hardware stores right now and about to ask the guy in the orange apron, "Excuse me, could you tell me where the drills are because I want to buy one". Yes, they may want one but for one reason only, because they need holes!

See the difference?

It's also important to understand the emotional aspect of sales and even more vital that you appreciate why people buy your product or service.

I'll give all my receipts and invoices to Lynda (she's our bookkeeper) and my accounts will go to Jared (he's our accountant) and everything will be alright because they both know what they are talking about and I won't have to worry.

I am paying not for their expertise but for the comfort, security and relaxed state I have, knowing all the 'numbers and tax stuff' is in the hands of people who know what they are doing.

And so it is with coaches and consultants. It's not your knowledge your clients are after, it's the peace of mind and security that knowledge brings with it. What you teach them will make them feel in control of that which hitherto had been out of control.

When you are selling it's probably not just the person seated in front of you.

When you are in a meeting with a prospect it might be that she loves what you have to offer and imagine that working with you would be well worthwhile but she'll have to justify that decision to use you to someone else within the organisation.

Of course, you'll know this because you'll have asked them who is involved in the decision-making process. (We will get on to questions later on in the book.)

So, everyone has to justify what they buy to at least two people: to themselves and then to someone close to them, whether that's a member of their family, a friend, a colleague, their boss or The Board.

You may meet with the CEO or CFO of an organisation and they warm to you and like the suggestions you are making about how you might help their business and think you're the person for the job!

However, they then have to feel confident enough about putting you in front of other members of the organisation, because if you are not good, it's not you who will get it in the neck: it's them.

The characteristics, attributes and qualities of good salespeople.

In addition to these visible or 'outward' characteristics, I'd like to draw your attention to some other, less visible, 'inward' traits that, in my opinion, salespeople also possess:

- Persistence
- They never ever stop developing business
- A positive attitude
- An aversion to hard work
- Belief in what they sell
- A definite but flexible focus

Persistence

Persistence means following up on every lead, contact and referral until it results in business, is put on hold for another time or is ditched indefinitely.

Persistence is about doing something to develop sales and business every day, no matter how small; whether that's an email, a phone call, a coffee, a letter, a LinkedIn message, attending a networking event or delivering a seminar.

They Never Ever Stop Developing Business

You must do at least one business development activity every day.

Never, ever, ever, ever, stop developing business. I have seen too many salespeople ease back when times were good. I worked with a firm once where I was specifically and repeatedly told to "take your foot off the gas regarding business development", a fact about which I felt most uncomfortable since I was responsible for sales. Four months later, I was taken to one side and told how disappointed management was that sales seemed to have not done as well as was expected!

I don't give a monkey's how busy you are, you must be able to look back at your day and know that you did at least one thing that would lead you to more sales.

It doesn't matter how small it is – send a brochure, follow up on a lead, ask someone for a referral or speak to someone outside the toilet on a train.

So, whatever you do, don't ever go to bed without being able to answer 'yes' to the question, "Did I do something to bring in another customer today?"

A Positive Attitude

Guess what; optimists are better at developing business than pessimists.

When a pessimist hears "No, thanks, we are really happy with our current supplier" they regard it as:

- Permanent – "If they won't buy what I have now then they won't ever buy it".
- Pervasive – "If they won't buy from me then no one will".
- Personal – "It's me! They didn't buy what I had because they didn't like me!"

An optimist just thinks: "Oh well, my timing's obviously not right, I'll make a note to get in touch with them in six months time. Right; on to my next prospect".

In fact, the optimist goes one step further. Having conceded that the timing is obviously not right, they tell the prospect that they'll leave them with the information they've been discussing and make a note in their diary – so the prospect can see them do it – that they will drop them a line in three or six months time.

Sales People Have an Aversion to Hard Work

Yes, they do.

Every salesperson I have ever met is at heart a lazy sod. (Why do you think they're in sales!) As long as you hit your targets, your time is pretty much your own when you're a sales rep. Lunch when you fancy it, start and end the day when you want and play loads of golf and declare it as 'client entertainment' or 'business development' or 'account management' on your timesheet!

But that does not mean they shy away from hard work or are not 100% dedicated to the cause. Far from it!

Salespeople are interested in selling as much stuff with the minimum amount of effort and in the shortest possible time frame, which means they don't work hard: they work smart!

Belief in What You Sell

It's very important to have belief in what you sell.

If you are currently working for an organisation or on your own and are attempting to persuade people to buy what you do or have and don't believe in either the product or organisation, then leave or stop now. I'm serious. You're wasting everyone's time.

I once worked for a radio station, employed to sell ads on air. In the three months I was there, I didn't sell one!

Why? I didn't like the station and, therefore, never listened to it!

Have a Definite and Flexible Focus

Good developers of business have a target. I don't just mean a figure, I mean a market. They know, before they set out in the morning, before they send the first email, write the first letter, send the first message or make the first telephone call, which organisations, in which sectors, they are going to contact.

They DO NOT think they can sell everything they have to offer to anyone.

However, because their income depends on being successful, they retain the flexibility to change targets if it becomes clear they can hit their monetary target more quickly.

The Model

This is the process we use at Tricres when developing a business. Conceived of, developed and refined by Nick since early 2008 and the method he has shared with countless thousands of people in the professional services sector.

- Stage One: TARGET
- Stage Two: CONNECT (Follow up and Keep control throughout the process)
- Stage Three: MEET
- Stage Four: ASK

A Quick Explanation

Stage One: TARGET – decide which sector, which organisation and in which geographical area and the individual(s) with whom you need to CONNECT.

Stage Two: CONNECT – you are looking to arrange to MEET (in person or virtually) the individual(s) who make the decision from whom to buy. Back in the day, when I was first taught selling, this person was the M.A.N. – the person with the Money, Authority and Need.

There are numerous ways to connect with these people:

- Email
- Phone
- Direct Message
- Via LinkedIn
- Letter
- In person (at a networking event, exhibition or conference)
- Third-party introduction

Stage Three: MEET – you then meet the decision maker(s), preferably in person because it's quicker and easier to establish rapport and begin building a relationship.

At this meeting, you are looking to ask questions in order to learn more about their business. You should be doing twice as much listening as talking.

Stage Four: ASK – unless, during the meeting, it becomes abundantly clear they do not need your services, it is incumbent on you to ALWAYS ask for the work/instruction/assignment!

Following Up and Keeping Control throughout the Process

This is fairly self-explanatory. You will find explanations and examples as you work through each step of the model over the following pages.

SCAN ME

Figure 3.1 Business Development for Business Coaches QR Code.

We cannot emphasise with sufficient emphasis just HOW IMPORTANT following up and keeping control is through the sales process.

It is, therefore, a theme we will point to throughout this book.

How to find clients who want to work with you and pay you for your services.

Stage One: TARGET

Getting started – a definite but flexible focus.

Why definite?

You must have a defined target market.

When first setting out to win business; it's tempting and reassuring to tell yourself there are loads of people to whom you could be selling your services. This, however, is a false sense of security and will have you doing lots of activity but with little reward. In other words, if you try and target everyone, you'll spread your activity too thin and achieve nothing.

Far too many people, in particular, those becoming self-employed, are so eager to get sales going they take a scatter-gun approach to sales and struggle as a consequence. They don't target their networking, advertising, sales calls or promotional material; taking the view that if they tell as many people as they can about what they have, they are bound to make sales.

It's a bit like packing your suitcase and showing up at the airport. You want to go away, because you need to unwind. You could, in theory, go anywhere to achieve that. So there you are, standing, staring at the departures board thinking, 'great, look at all the places I can go!'

But you can only go one place at a time and if you haven't decided where, you'll not know which departure gate to go to. This means you'll wander around the airport, wasting lots of time and energy but not actually getting very far!

However, if you know your ultimate destination, then you know where to target your effort!

It's no different when developing business. You need to make lots of effort to hit the target you've chosen but you can only hit one or maybe two, with any real impact, at the same time.

Why flexible?

'Flexible': because whilst you need to set out with your eye on a specific target, you also need to be flexible enough to adapt if you're not getting the results you need or had anticipated.

At the end of the day, you sell to make money and if you aren't making money from your target market, you need to pick another one. And sometimes, although you set off in one direction opportunities in an area you had never considered arise, in which case, grab them!

It's also a whole lot easier and more effective to establish a great reputation within one specialist field than try and be all things to all sectors because even when you do concentrate all your energies in one sector, be that geographical, professional or industrial, you will inevitably be asked to do work in others.

Take MASSIVE action!

If you are new to coaching and consulting with no paying clients, you are going to have to take MASSIVE action in order to generate momentum and begin earning.

If you have a large amount of cash and/or a partner who can take the financial strain whilst you are getting started, then you may feel you can relax a little, which is a nice position to be in. In which case, perhaps it's merely 'ACTION' you need to take?!

The first thing you do is make a list: a physical list. If you like a spread on a computer use that, if you prefer pen and paper, likewise but you NEED a list!

Your target list.

Who should be on it?

Everyone with whom you have a business relationship and preferably the M.A.N. – the person with the Money, Authority and Need. The decision maker!

Once you have captured all those names, you then need to sort them according to the strength of your relationship.

- HOT
- WARM
- COLD
- TEPID

Those people who are 'HOT' should be at the top of your list because you're going to approach them first.

The reason they are first is because they view you as being credible and trust you. Trust and credibility are the two ingredients necessary if you are to ever influence or persuade someone.

BTW: Once you have listed your business relationships according to temperature, it's well worth while conducting the same exercise with regard to friends and family because although they might not be on your target list in terms of working in the sectors you wish to approach, they may know people who do and would probably be more than willing to help!

HOT: This market is made up of people and organisations that already buy your services or products and with whom you have an existing relationship.

This will be the case if you have recently left employment and are now setting out on your own.

If there exists an agreement between your former employer you may not contact clients within a certain period of time, within a defined geographical area, you must abide by that. There's no point annoying those you may hope to do business with in the future.

Of course, that doesn't preclude them from contacting you! Know doubt you will announce, on the relevant social media platforms your new venture, making it easier for your business contacts to congratulate and message you!

WARM: This market is populated by former clients with whom you did business fairly recently but aren't 'live'. It would also include people to whom you have been recommended and perhaps even made contact with you. They are a 'warm' contact but a 'hot' lead!

TEPID/LUKEWARM: This is kind of 'catch-all' market, which may comprise the following:

- People with whom you have not done business for quite a while (perhaps years) but are not 'Cold' because they do/did know you.
- Clients of former colleagues
- Referrals

The first two are self-explanatory so let's take a look at referrals.

Referrals

Referrals are people who would otherwise be cold but for the recommendation of someone who has, in effect, 'warmed them up'.

They work in two ways.

1. You have a firm on your target list and ask an existing client/contact if they know the person responsible for commissioning coaching and consulting and if they do, whether they would help by affording you an introduction – normally via email.
2. You ask a very good client if they could think of any firms that you should be approaching and if they could facilitate an introduction.

It goes without saying you must have a very good relationship in order for (1) to be successful but even more so in the case of (2).

A referral acts as a cosy little heater to warm up otherwise cold contacts.

Referrals are only something that will bring results once you have established a solid working and often, friendship-type relationship with your client, so in the early days of your business development activity you might have to rely on a great deal more cold calling.

Referrals are how tradespeople get the majority of their work and you will too, once you've started making a name for yourself.

COLD: 'Cold calling'

When we began selling in the late 80s/early 90s, there were only two ways you could connect with a cold contact - send a letter or telephone them.

Both still have their advantages.

There are 'cold' calls and 'freezing cold' calls.

Cold calls are to organisations that are in the market which you are currently operating in and know lots about.

If you are working in a relatively small market, in a relatively small geographical area, the chances are your existing clients or customers will know people within the same sector.

So when you contact a firm without the benefit of an introduction to warm them up, always mention the names of firms you already deal with and more importantly the names of the individual CEOs/Department Heads, working on the principal there's a fair chance they'll know them!

You should name drop too because it's very effective at persuading people to do things, like meet you. The phenomenon is known as 'Social Proof'.

Before listing those firms in your cold, as opposed to 'freezing' market, ask yourself these questions:

1. In which markets or sectors do I work at the moment?
2. Do I make money in those markets?
3. Do I like working in those markets?
4. Do I work with everyone within those sectors?

If the answer to (2) and (3) is 'yes' but it's a big fat 'no' to (4), then that's where you want to be targeting.

Freezing Cold

Those people who have no idea you exist because they operate in a market completely outside the one in which you are established, fall into this last category and are, therefore, the very hardest to tackle.

If you are doing your targeting properly, in other words tackling existing customers, using referrals and building your profile within those markets, as well as tackling your cold market, then dipping into the freezing bit should be totally unnecessary. Unless, of course, you are brand new to a market, in which case you are going to do some serious cold calling.

Once you become established and assuming you are doing a good job, you should find you make very few calls to drum up business because word of mouth takes over and people are recommending you to others all over the place.

Summary

A note about keeping your hot clients hot – showing the love/what else can you help them with and referrals.

Bottom line: don't waste your time going after new clients until you are sure your existing ones know about all that you do and that it would be in their interest to buy it from you.

Example

A few years back the CEO of a large firm in the Midlands told me that his firm had lost a client. When he asked the Managing Director of the company why they were no longer using his firm's services, he replied, "Because you don't love us anymore".

When the CEO asked him to illuminate he told him that when the firm were originally looking to win his business, they had been told that they were special, that they were beautiful and lovely and that they would treasure their business and work hard to keep things just so. But that as the years had gone on, they had gradually stopped paying them as much attention to a point where they now felt that their business was being taken for granted.

All the while, the magic and sparkle was fading, another, rival firm had been gently wooing and courting the CEOs client. This new firm had told them that they were beautiful, special and lovely and they would be showered with attention and love.

So, guess what: yep, they went with the competitor.

Don't ever take your clients for granted. They need to know they are still desired. Sending emailed articles and newsletters doesn't count!! How loved would you feel if your partner kept in touch via a newsletter!

Look at these figures concerning the reasons why people stop buying: they are really interesting:

- 1% die
- 3% move away
- 5% follow a friend's or relative's recommendation
- 9% find an alternative they perceive to be better quality or value
- 14% are dissatisfied with the product or service
- 68% leave because of indifference. They go elsewhere because they don't feel valued or loved!

A Salutary Tale

A number of years back a very large law firm that had been acting on behalf of Honda (UK) was unceremoniously dumped by the firm. This event was front page news in The Lawyer magazine and within the article was a comment from Honda, citing the principal reason for their decision to look elsewhere for legal services; apparently, they were a tad affronted by the fact that the 'Client Relationship Partner' responsible for the Honda account did not know where the company's UK head office was!

Once you have written down your target list you then need to start to contact each one in turn and find out who it is you need to MEET but before you do that, you're going to have to CONNECT with them earlier on I made reference to the M.A.N.

Nick was first introduced to this 'person' when he was taught how to sell back in 1987. The person with the Money, Authority and Need.

When we say 'CONNECT', we refer to communication with the individual, whether that be via phone, email or letter but even then we don't simply mean 'making them aware of your existence and what you are offering' but making an emotional connection* with them.

Throughout the book you will see numerous letters and Emails that Nick has sent during the business development process and a common theme running through them all is making just such an emotional connection, however, more of that later.

Of course, there is one forum in which you can CONNECT and MEET simultaneously, and that's networking.

You can read all about that subject later on in the book but for now, we want to give you some pointers on how to contact people directly and CONNECT.[1]

Stage Two: CONNECT

In order for you to see the entire process, we are going to take you through the steps we take when contacting someone in our cold market; when we have only the name of the organisation I wish to approach.

The great thing about 'going in cold' is that you get to choose!

It's a blank sheet! Pick who you want, which sectors, which organisations and where they are in the country, Europe, and the globe! But choose you must!

You must not and cannot take the view, "Well, I can sell my product to everyone because everyone is a potential purchaser of my product".

One, because with the very odd exception, that's not true, and two, because that's a big target you're aiming at which means you will spread your sales efforts too thin.

It makes sense, however, to pick a market with which you are most familiar. So whilst you are going to have to make cold calls, at least they won't be in a freezing market.

Cold calling is every salesperson's nightmare. In fact, one of the selling points for your double-glazing sales rep ads or conservatory ads is if the firm can boast a ready supply of leads because even the hardest of salespeople baulk at the thought of cold calling.

Should you find yourself having to break into new markets in which you have no contacts then here's what you should do.

Step One

First of all, break your target market down into a geographical area – if you want to make appointments to see your new prospects then it makes sense to tackle those within a defined area.

Then make a list of the firms in which you have an interest, using criteria in order to narrow them down. When Nick opted to go for the legal market he went online and looked at something called 'The Legal 500' for the UK, which details the top 500 firms in, guess where…the UK.

This fantastic resource then separates these firms by geographical location and he decided to plump for London. One, because he likes London and two because he already knew the biggest law firms were located there and figured big firms would have big training budgets and lots of lawyers that would need training.

He made note of the top 20 law firms, their postal and website addresses, and phone numbers. He also made a note of how many lawyers they had and whether they had any other offices in the UK.

He then rang each one in turn and that's exactly what you should do – methodically and systematically.

Step Two

Ask yourself what you want from the call.

In fact, don't bother. There is only one reason you are making this call: in order to arrange to MEET the other person.

You want to meet them in order to have a chat, find out what they do, how they go about sourcing/choosing whatever it is you are offering and to see whether what you are selling might be of use to them. That's it.

Step Three

Go somewhere private.

Making a telephone call to someone you don't know is not a spectator sport. It's something to be done in private, away from others and whilst standing up and quite possibly pacing about the room.

Standing up will make you feel more confident and speak more clearly.

Step Four

You might be worried the first call is really hard but worry not: it's dead easy.

All you want to get from the first call is the name and title of the person who is responsible for buying what it is you're selling.

In Nick's case, he wanted to find out who was responsible for training and development along with a few simple but really important details:

- Their full job title – 'Head of Learning and Development' or was it 'Director of Training and Learning'?
- Their title – 'Ms, Miss, Mrs, Dr, Mr', etc.
- Their full name – ALWAYS ASK HOW YOU SPELL THEIR NAME.

In practice it sounds like this:

You: Good morning. I wonder if you could help* me, I'm trying to find out the name of the person who is responsible for training and development within the firm. I don't need to speak to them but just need their name.

Them: Yes, can I ask what it's regarding?

You: Sure, I need to send them something in the post.

*Help – Get into the habit of using this word whenever you are developing a business. We use it ALL the time and the reason is simple: it's very difficult for a person to say 'no' to a request for help.

It has to be said that it's rare that anyone will ask us what it's regarding. Most of the time they'll provide the name of the person and then it's just left for us to check the details listed above.

If you are a 'cold call' virgin, YOU DO NOT WANT TO TALK TO THEM AT THIS POINT – even if the receptionist or secretary has asked you if you'd like to be put through.

You are going to call them when you are good and ready and in the correct state of mind and being put through when you have not prepared is never a good idea.

But why not ask to get put straight through when you first call and find out the name of the person you want to see?

One of the roles of receptionists and secretaries is to act as a kind of 'gatekeeper' to their colleagues within the office. Every organisation receives countless calls a day from sales reps and if everyone was put through the fear is that no work would get done and so those at the front line, taking the calls, are there to filter out the rubbish.

Additionally, if you call and ask for the name of the training and development manager, it's clear you don't know them and am cold calling!

So wait a day (if you phone too soon after your initial 'fact-finding' call, there's a good chance they will recognise your voice and realise you are selling something.)

By the way, if, when you call, the person you talk to offers more information than you were after, do take it! So they ask if you'd like the training and development manager's direct dial number or email address, say "Yes please" and thank them for their help.

Of course, once you've made a few calls and are comfortable with your patter, by all means, accept their offer to put you through. (Although, always have dates to hand – more of that later.)

So, once you have their details make a note of them and then phone a day or so later. If the organisation has more than one office, check at which one your 'contact' is located.

Research

Go on LinkedIn and find out about them and their background.

A look at their company website will probably reveal more about their role within the organisation and who works with them.

By all means, do some research but what you need can be done in five minutes. Don't start using it as an excuse to avoid making the calls!

Step Five

There are times when it's better to call than others and all we'd say is; think about the times of day when you really could do without a phone call and assume that other people are just the same because they are.

So never call first thing in the morning – especially on a Monday.

It takes most of us an hour or so to settle into the working day. We need a tea or coffee, to open the mail, take a look at our inbox and maybe just catch up on stuff with immediate colleagues.

We call people between about 10.30 and 11.30 or 2.30 and about 4.30 but always, always ask the person whether it's a bad time to be speaking to them.

A quick note here…

Notice we have not asked whether it's a 'good time'. This is deliberate and here's why.

You have been approached by people in the street, asking if you have a minute, so they might tell you about a charity of which they are trying to sign you up for a regular, monthly donation.

Your answer is normally a rushed, very polite, 'no thanks, I am in a hurry'.

Imagine, if next time, you replied 'yes' to the question 'Have you got a minute?'

Now what?

You are now stopped. The charity rep is telling you about the wonderful work their organisation does and you are thinking:

How long is this REALLY going to take?

> I know I am being sold too!
> How am I going to say 'no' without sounding callous and heartless?
> Oh, why on earth did I say 'yes': this is really awkward!

You see, the charity rep wants to hear 'yes'. In the same way, when you get through to the M.A.N. on the telephone, you do too!

And whilst 'yes' is a nice sound for you, it may be the catalyst for the same thoughts you had when you replied in the affirmative to the charity collector!

However, if you phrase the questions, when put through to the M.A.N. 'is now a bad time to talk?' Their reply 'no' makes them feel safe. Saying 'no' is like putting up a forcefield through which no salesperson can penetrate.

And because they feel safe, they are likely to be more relaxed. And when people feel relaxed they tend to open up more!

It's a little technique that's terribly effective. Try it!

We must confess we have to be in the mood to make the initial call to the person we wish to arrange a meeting with but one thing's for sure, no matter how many times we've done it we always feel a bit nervy so don't worry if you do too: it's normal.

What we can say, however, is once you have made a call which results in you getting through to the person and securing a date to meet up; you'll be elated and it's then easy to quickly whizz through the rest of the people on your list.

That's one of the reasons we suggest you list the names of all the people you want to speak to, so you can go through them really quickly and establish a nice rhythm and momentum.

Furthermore, once you have one in the diary, you can mention that on your subsequent call. Remember what we said earlier about social proof? If the person you are calling knows their opposite number at a firm in the same sector in the same area is seeing you, then they feel far more inclined to meet you too; not wishing to 'miss out'. Fabulous!

Step Six (and the Gorgeously Lovely 'Alternative Close')

You've probably heard the term 'closing' in the context of selling. It's a word that many associate with the very cleverest and cunning of salespeople who can call on all manner of weird and wonderful ploys in order to get unsuspecting, innocent folk to part with cash for things they don't really want.

However, what it really means is getting commitment, which is why many people in sales have dropped the term 'closing' in favour of the far more lovely phrase 'getting/securing commitment or sealing the deal'.

Personally, we don't think it matters and therefore use both as the mood takes us.

Let's assume the person you want to speak to is Roger Moore.

Before making this call you MUST have three dates to offer him; two close together and another one a few weeks later, in case he is away on hols or something. For the purposes of this example, we'll go for the 4th or 5th or the 23rd.

DO NOT get put through to Roger and then ask, "So, when would it be most convenient?"

There are two reasons you should never do this:

1. It hands control over to him. He is free to say any day he chooses, "April the 17th is good for me". In which case you're stuffed.
2. It makes it difficult for him to make a decision. Contrary to popular belief, we don't like too much choice because when faced with limitless options we find it difficult to choose just one.

By offering Roger a choice between alternatives, you make it easy for him to choose. All he has to do is look at two adjacent pages in his diary, rather than trawl through umpteen.

This method of getting people to commit is known as the 'ALTERNATIVE CLOSE' in the sales world and is highly effective when wanting to secure dates for meetings and appointments.

Of course, if Roger says he is out of the office on the 4th and 5th, then you can offer him the 23rd.

DO NOT BE TOO AVAILABLE! Don't ever say, "Well, I'm free for the next 3 weeks", or "I'm free pretty much anytime that suits you". Such phrases tell your caller that you aren't busy and may leave them thinking, "'He can't be that good, or he'd be busy".'

One of the things that make people or objects desirable is scarcity.

When you are setting this meeting up, make sure you mention other firms and organisations you are meeting with.

"Mm, let's see, I could do the 23rd because I'm in your neck of the woods on the 22nd seeing Shell and the BBC". You get the picture.

Let's say Roger picks the 5th. You then offer him another alternative:

You: Morning or afternoon best for you?
Roger: Morning would be better.

We then move it on to pining down a time and although we'll still continue offering alternatives.

So, continue with:

You: 10.15 or 11.15?

If someone suggests 10 am for a meeting: how long will the meeting last:

- An hour?
- 10.30, ½ an hour?
- 10.15, 15 minutes or 45 minutes?

Nick prefers to set up meetings for 15 minutes past or to the hour because people will assume that it'll all be done within 45 minutes, which it normally is.

We know this seems silly but it works and sends a strong but almost subliminal message to the person you wish to see that you aren't going to waste their time (and, from their point of view, even if you did, you'd have only wasted 45 minutes of it rather than a whole hour).

There's a quirkiness about it as well; it sort of unsettles people ever so slightly; a phenomenon known as 'cognitive dissonance', which is a fancy phrase for 'that's a bit odd'.

Want to experience even more dissonance?

Imagine someone suggesting you meet at 10.03 or 3.22.

So, don't go for 'weird' times and really unsettle people but try suggesting quarter or twenty past or quarter or twenty to and see how you get on.

Arriving early for meetings is always good practice, although turning up at reception 15 minutes early is, probably too much.

Finally – always, always confirm right away with an email. Something along these lines is nice:

'Hi Roger, good to chat with you a moment ago and just to confirm that we are meeting up at 10.15 on Monday the 5th of August at Starbucks on Holborn just by City Thames Link station. I look forward to seeing you then.

OK, Back to Step Six

You make the call, it is answered and you ask to be put through to 'Roger'.

If there is more than one person with that name working there then they'll ask, "Which one?" To which you say "Roger, Roger Moore".

The point is that when you ask for Roger Moore, you should say it in a way that gives the impression that you've known him for years.

We reckon we get put straight through to the person we want 50% of the time, simply by sounding authoritative and matter-of-fact – as though we speak to our 'contact' every day of the week.

The other 50% of the time you'll get asked, "What is it regarding?" In which case, you must reply honestly and say, "I want to arrange to pop in and see him".

It's vital you are upfront about your motives here and you focus on what it is you wish to achieve, namely, an appointment to see the person.

Half the time, the receptionist will put you through to the PA rather than the person you asked for. In this case, you'll need to go through the following step – Step Seven.

Step Seven (Getting Past Their P.A.)

Personal assistants, secretaries and executive assistants are great people with whom to strike up a relationship because if they like you, they'll go out of their way to get you in front of their boss.

In the early days of establishing his training business, Nick spent three months trying to secure a meeting with the head of learning and development of a leading national law firm, only to have every request – via email, telephone and letter ignored.

Each time he called he ended up talking to his P.A., who, over those 12 weeks, he got to know quite well. It got to a point where not only did she feel sorry for him but thought her boss was rude for not having acknowledged him, so she sent him an email (and copied Nick in!) in an amusing but quite forthright style, telling him that she thought he'd been impolite and that he should contact him immediately to set up a meeting – which he promptly did!

The thing to bear in mind with people in their position is not to give them a load of bullshit or, far worse, take an arrogant or dismissive tone. Not only is it ignorant but commercially stupid: P.A.s know more about their bosses' diaries than the boss does! And what's more, if she doesn't like you, you don't stand a chance of ever getting to see her boss.

If you get put through to a P.A. or secretary this is how the conversation normally flows:

P.A: Hello, Roger Moore's office. How can I help you?
You: Hi, is Roger in the office this morning?
P.A: Can I ask what it's regarding?
You: Yes, I'm trying to fix up a time to meet up with him for a coffee.
P.A: Will he know what it's regarding?
You: No, he'll have no idea, we've never met before, which is why I want to pop in and see him.

I'm a former lawyer but now spend my time teaching lawyers from the very junior to senior level in a range of communication skills and I wanted to find out how Roger goes about co-ordinating and organising training within the firm and to see whether what I do might be of help. I'm seeing Freshfields on the 3rd and A&O on the 4th and wondered if he was free on either the 5th or 6th?

It's been our experience that secretaries and P.A.s will appreciate your candour and therefore be quite helpful in suggesting how you are best to go about securing a meeting.

At this point, she will either suggest that you send information:

P.A: Do you have a brochure?
You: Yes, would you like me to send him a copy.
P.A: Yes, that would be useful and then I can pass it on to him.
You: Great. Shall I mark it for your attention or his?

Or put you straight through.

We've reproduced a couple of letters that Nick wrote in response to such a request. The first one is when the PA asked him to send the information to her. The second is when she asked him to address it to her boss.

However, before we do that we want to stop for a moment and talk about letters in general.

The Letter

Nick sent a great number of letters when first getting his business off the ground and these were a major plank of his business development activity.

He sent them at every possible opportunity because apart from standing up and speaking they are the single most effective way of CONNECTING with people.

And NO ONE ELSE WRITES THEM ANYMORE!

If you want to stand out and have a chance of winning business then you MUST stop doing what all your competitors are doing and do something different.

However, there may be a number of reasons you prefer not to send an email: fine. That's up to you. It's your coaching and consulting business you're trying to establish.

The point is, whether a LinkedIn message, email or letter, what you send MUST be engaging, set you apart from the banal dross most people send and afford them an insight into the kind of person you are.

You want to give them sufficient information they think, "Yes, I'm prepared to spend half an hour finding out more about the bloke/woman. I'd like to meet the person behind this message. They sound interesting".

However, there are some themes running through the vast majority of them. What follows is a fairly typical letter, with an analysis at the end of it.

> Hello Alison
>
> My name's Nick and I co-founded Tricres.
>
> I used to be a lawyer but turned away from the 'Dark Side' some years ago and now, rather ironically but nevertheless, appropriately, spend my time training and coaching lawyers at all levels, from countries across the globe, on how to network, present, pitch, influence and develop business.
>
> Although I live in Edinburgh most of my work is with firms in London. In fact, I suspect that I may be the only person in Scotland with an Oyster Card on automatic top-up! I work for firms such as Freshfields, A&O, Olswang, BLP and a whole bunch of others.
>
> I last spoke about training on a visit to your offices at 45 High Street, where I met Sally Brown but that was 18 months ago and you were with a different firm and so was I. So what I'd dearly like to do now is pop in and see you find out how you go about training and whether what I do might be of help.
>
> I shall give you a bell in a week and see if we can put a date in the diary.
>
> Regards
> Nick

OK, let's take this apart.

One rule though – one page of A4 only.

Two pages are too fiddly. Reading two pages is too much like hard work. If you cannot fit it all on one side then reduce your font to 10 (no smaller) and if it still doesn't fit, then take some words out.

Paragraphs:

- A quick and friendly introduction
- Credibility – Nick was a lawyer, he worked with lawyers all the time from all over the world and he's busy
- Credibility – These are major players in your sector. If they use me, I'm probably worth meeting.
- The background and the reason for contacting you.
- What I'm going to do next and when.

COMPLIMENT SLIPS AND 'LITERATURE', which accompanies the letter

Emailing a brochure or information about the services you offer is all very well, but let's be honest when was the last time you were sent a brochure via email and actually read it – all the way through?!

Put simply, people can't be bothered opening up brochures with that stupid 'Adobe Acrobat' thingy that seems to be in constant need of updates.

And let me tell you how adamant we are about this – even if someone asks us to email a copy of our 'literature' we tell them we'd prefer they had a real copy because, we are human beings. Human beings do like having their senses stimulated – touch, sight, smell and sound and you only get one of those with an email but four with the real thing.

Send the information on what you do, in the post. You want them to literally get a 'feel' for what it is you do.

Rebecca and Nick, along with their head of brand and design, Lauren, spent hours and hours developing our branding, brochures, workbooks and booklets.

We sweated over layout, colours and even the type and quality of the paper we should use because we wanted people to handle it, open it and see what was inside.

Right, back to the letters in response to the secretaries' requests.

Letter One

Hi Andrea

I hope your hen weekend went well and you enjoyed Rose Street to the full!

You'll find some info enclosed about what I do, which will give you a flavour of the kind of stuff I do.

I am in the north-west seeing a few law firms on Friday the 25th of June and would like to pop in and have a chat with Cris and you, to find out more about your firm and how you go about training the people within your business and whether what I do might be of help.

Cris will no doubt be snowed under with emails when she comes back so I'll probably wait until Thursday to give you a ring.

Thanks a lot
Nick

Letter Two

Good morning, Jane

I've just come off the phone having talked to Aileen (I do hope it's 'Aileen' and not 'Eileen' – sorry if I misheard.)

Well, she was really friendly and dead helpful and said she'd pass a message on to you to say I'd called and that I wanted to arrange to meet with you to chat about training.

I'm a former lawyer who turned away from the 'Dark Side' some years ago but now earns a living, training and coaching trainees to senior partners in communication skills. Over the past 12 months, I've worked with loads of law firms (there's a nice list in the blurb) and have been lucky enough to have won 'The LETG Trainer of the Year 07/08' www.letg.org.uk.

Anyway, of late I keep hearing the names of Dublin-based law firms – including yours – and learning about the really great work they are doing but also the way in which they look after their people and I thought it was about time I got in touch and found out more. (The fact that it's £4.99 from Edinburgh to Dublin with Ryanair also helps!)

So, what I'd like to do is pop in and see you, hear more about your firm and the way you go about delivering training and whether what I do might be of help at some point.

Take a look at my stuff, which will give you a flavour of what I'm all about and I'll give you a call on Friday to see if we can set something up.

Thanks a lot
Nick

Step Eight – When You Get Through to the M.A.N.

You need to keep this short, sweet and to the point. Sure, it may turn out there is an opportunity for small talk, in which case be prepared to indulge in a little, but whatever you do, do not waste Roger's time.

We all know what it's like to be at the end of a sales call: sometimes you'll chat a bit and other times you just want rid of them ASAP and it's even more annoying when people don't get to the point.

Getting to the point

You will develop a bit of a 'script' of sorts once you've done this a few times but whatever form of words you opt for make sure you KEEP IT RELAXED AND LIGHT!

What you say might go like this:

You: Hi Roger, I understand that you're the person responsible for learning and development for the firm? Is that right?

Roger: Yes, I am.

You: Thank goodness for that! Is now a bad time for you to speak?

Roger: No. I can spare a couple of minutes.

If he says, "No, it's not ideal, I'm just about to go into a meeting", tell him that you'll call back and offer a couple of alternatives

Assuming he answers "yes", then continue…

You: My name's Nick, Nick Davies and I used to be a lawyer but turned away from the dark side some years ago and now spend my time travelling up and down the country teaching lawyers in a range of communication skills. The reason I'm calling is I'd really like to pop in and see you, find out more about the firm, how you go about training your lawyers in those kinds of skills and see whether what I do might be of help. I'm in London on the 4th and 5th and since you're the first person I've called, you can choose which one's best for you.

THEN SHUT UP and wait for him to answer! DO NOT KEEP TALKING.

If he asks you questions, then answer them but DO NOT GO IN TO LOTS OF DETAIL AND DON'T EVEN THINK ABOUT 'SELLING' OVER THE PHONE!!!!!!!

It takes 32 seconds to have that conversation – I've just timed it!

Even though it's very quick, I want you to notice what you are attempting to get across in such a short space of time.

Let's look at it point by point:

- Clarify that he is the right person to talk to.
- Introduce yourself and repeat your name.
- Give him a brief insight into your background and – in terms of teaching lawyers – increase your credibility.
- Humour, 'Dark Side'. This works because many Learning and Development managers are former lawyers and even if they aren't, they do understand that working with them brings some unique difficulties. It also shows you are not taking yourself too seriously.
- 'Travelling up and down the country'. Factually correct but signals that you're busy and probably have a lot of experience working with many different law firms.
- 'The reason I'm calling'. Straight to the point!
- 'Find out about your firm and see whether what I do might be of help'. You are interested in finding out about what he does, but you are ultimately hoping he might use your services – in other words, you are coming to sell to him, albeit in a very gentle, no-pressure kind of way.
- 'I'm in London on the 4th and 5th' – the alternative close. But also indicates that you intend to be busy enough to fill two days with appointments.
- 'You are the first person I've called'. I'm ringing a number of firms but someone's got to be first – again, just a little light humour. (If you have other meetings arranged or are in the process of arranging them with other firms, then you will make a point of telling him the names of these organisations – see below.)

This 'script' works for Nick and although not every call he makes is the same, he pretty much sticks to it.

You need to develop your own script, in the same way you develop your own style when writing a letter or email.

The point, however, is that you get a bit of your personality across in addition to telling them why you wish to meet up. It will take you a good few calls before you settle on a form of words you feel comfortable with but it will happen – trust us.

If you have one or two appointments already

If, when you called Roger, you already had one or two appointments in the diary, mention that fact when you spoke to him.

"I'm in London on the 4th and 5th, seeing Patrick McCann at Links, Stephanie Willabon-Hill at Bristows and Phillipa Smith at Pinsent Masons was hoping to pop in and see you as well".

Two things here:

1. Other people in your position in your sector think it's worth meeting me (the inference being – you should too – SOCIAL PROOF).
2. Credibility – 'If these people have agreed to see him, I might as well'.

Mention the names of individuals because there is a good chance that within a particular sector, within a particular city, people occupying the role of Head of Learning and Development will know each other and may have some kind of formal or informal network (which, in the case of Learning and Development in law firms, they do!).

What if they ask questions?

Once you have got through to someone, the chances are they will ask questions and whilst you should answer them honestly and efficiently, you should NOT go into detail because you'll end up selling over the phone and that's difficult and best to be avoided.

Here are some of the questions you may get asked and here's how you handle them.

Question: Could you tell me what other services you offer?

Answer: We offer a range of commercial legal services to clients, including mergers and acquisitions, financing, construction and employment. I'll be able to explain in more detail when we meet up. Is Tuesday or Wednesday best?

Question: Do you have experience of asset finance work in the shipping sector.

Answer: We have a great deal of experience in many areas, including some shipping-related work. When we meet next week I'll be able to tell you more about what we do.

Question: Could you tell me what you charge?

Answer: It depends on what type of work we are undertaking and what level of service you require. That's the sort of thing we can have a natter about when we meet up. Is Monday morning or afternoon best?

As you can see, you are acknowledging their question, whilst simultaneously avoiding going into detail and closing – the 'alternative' in your replies to the first and third questions, and the assumptive in the second.

Experience tells us price questions are those that people fear most: although they needn't be. In fact, they should be cherished because any enquiry regarding price is what is referred to as a 'buying sign'.

Someone with no interest whatsoever in purchasing your service doesn't care less what you charge.

Price

Talking confidently about how much you charge for your services is an important point, which is covered in the chapter 'How Much do I Charge?' on page 136. We wish to There's more discount to be had!

However, what we will point out is discussions about money should, wherever possible, be conducted face to face.

Below is an example of how Nick dealt with a query regarding costs, which was raised via email.

The Background

Nick had made a cold telephone call the day before and spoken to a training administrator who had gone to see if she could put him through to Sue.

She'd come back to tell him Sue was busy, happy with her current suppliers and not available on Monday but could Nick drop some information off when he was visiting Bristol the following week.

Normally he would have done just that because it gives him an opportunity to ask to see the person when he goes to their offices, see their reception, get a feel for the firm and pick up some corporate brochures.

However, he was dubious that she was not in on Monday (he just got a feeling he was being fobbed off) and so wanted to send her the stuff right away so if she changed her mind, she could make space for him on Monday.

So, he wrote her a letter and posted it the same day. This is what it said:

> Good morning, Sue
>
> I have just come off the phone, having spoken to Ruth, who very kindly let me know that you are the person who deals with training and development within the firm. I know she mentioned to you I was in Bristol on the 11th and it's a shame you are busy that day: it would have been nice to learn more about Ogilvy, what you do in the way of training and whether what I do might be of help.
>
> Anyway, she said I should pop in and drop some info off next Monday but I've opted to use the post – just so you get it sooner.
>
> So, you'll find a biog of me, which will give you a little feel for my background, along with the outlines of the four principal courses I do and a little info on what else I do and my style.
>
> Ruth did say that you do have training suppliers you are happy with, and to be honest I'd have been amazed if you hadn't. And, assuming you are happy with them, it would be daft for you to look elsewhere.
>
> However, things change and you may come across a training need that's not covered, or is a bit quirky, or you need someone who can speak at an away day or conference, or maybe you just feel it's time to get a different perspective, then at least you know a bit more about how I can help.

> I will leave things with you and drop you a line or give you a call in four months, just to keep in touch and in case things have changed. Other than that, I'll not bother you again.
>
> Thanks a lot, Sue

Sue replied via email.

> Good morning, Nick
>
> #
>
> Thanks for your introductory information – it makes a real pleasure to read someone's "blurb" and find yourself smiling!!
>
> You've given me a very clear picture of who you are and what you're about – my immediate question is "If I were to engage your services how much would it cost me?"
>
> Given that you're based in Scotland but are in Bristol on Monday, if I feel your fees are within reach (I try and get everything I can for next to nothing as any good buyer does, whilst expecting the best quality!). I'd be happy to make time on Monday 11th to see you if that's OK with you.
>
> I look forward to hearing from you. Sorry, I haven't got time to call you instead of sending this email – I'm a victim of my diary this week I'm afraid.
>
> Regards
> Sue

My Reply, via email.

> Glad you like the blurb, Sue.
>
> Talking about money via email is so horrid, isn't it? And if you think I can help you make your fee earners better at winning business and I think it would be lovely to work with you, then I don't think we would allow price to get in the way: it never has with any other client.
>
> Let's meet up and have a natter about it.
>
> However, you can be rest assured that I am, as they say in the L'Oreal ads 'worth it'.

Getting into a discussion about price over the phone with someone you have never met and have never seen what you do is a waste of time, doing it via email is even worse (there's no pitch, tone, pace, volume, intonation or emotion in an email).

If Nick had given Sue a price via email she would have absolutely no way of knowing whether what he was selling was worth it! Fine, when selling a product you can send her an example of it in the post! But when selling a service, whilst she can get an idea of what Nick covered by looking at his brochure or having a gander at the website; there's no substance to it: no flesh on the bones!

There are lots of coaches and consultants offering their services at more or less the same kind of price you are. The person you seek to persuade has to MEET you.

The difference between you and your competitors is what you do, how you deliver it and how you bring it to life.

The best thing for Sue to do is see Nick in action. However, because that's not possible, the next best thing is to meet him and, gain a sense of who he is.

During that meeting, she will do two things; first, see if she gets on with him and reckons he's the type of bloke she could work with, and second, we would suggest, more importantly, decide whether he's the sort of person she could put in front of her fellow directors and mangers.

And here's the thing; notwithstanding she may reckon he is the best thing since sliced bread, if she's not confident her colleagues will like him, that's it; it won't go any further because if she puts him in front of them and they don't like him, it's not Nick who will get it in the neck: it's her!

When you do get questions or queries regarding price, by all means, say something along the following lines:

"Well, it depends on what level of service you want, the length and complexity of the job and the seniority of the person who's best suited to deal with it but we can talk more about that when we meet up. Now, when's best for you, the third or fourth?"

But avoid, where at all possible, discussions other than those conducted face to face.

What happened?

Sue and Nick met up in Bristol and got on like a house on fire. At the end of the meeting, they agreed that whilst there was nothing he could help her within the immediate future, they would keep in touch and Nick would call her in six months' time. (He set up the FOLLOW UP before leaving her office.)

When he called again, she'd left. He asked the receptionist where she had gone and who had taken over her role.

Nick contacted the new person and tracked Sue down. He then secured the original prospect company as a client and Sue's new firm as well! Brilliant!

It's great when people move on because you then get two people to FOLLOW UP with and guess what?

When Sue, in common with everyone else, moved into her new role at her new employer, she conducted a thorough and comprehensive review of all the firm's suppliers, as did her successor. And that, ladies and gentlemen is THE perfect time to be getting in touch – because that's when people are looking to make changes and get new suppliers in.

Nobody, but nobody, arrives new in the post and says, "I think I'll just keep things exactly as the previous person had them".

It is also why you should be seeking to establish and build relationships with lots of people within the same firm, so that when a new decision maker comes on board and they are conducting a thorough and comprehensive review when they ask their team, 'What's Nick like?' they'll say good things and by implication that you are credible and can be trusted. In other words, they will act as your internal referees.

You detect reluctance

Sometimes, when you phone people out of the blue and try to arrange to see them, you'll begin to detect a hesitancy or reluctance in their voice during the conversation. You'll get the distinct impression they are asking you questions as a way of being polite because they really don't wish to see you.

Should this be the case, then be sensitive to it. Don't roll over straight away – keep coming back to the dates when you can see them, as we've detailed above – however, if you sense you have pushed it enough, take the initiative and therefore the pressure off them and say something along these lines:

You: Would be easier to just send you something in the post so you can get a better feel for what I do?

What's amazing is that as soon as you say this they immediately relax because you've articulated what they were thinking Normally you'll get a...

Roger: Oh, do you mind? That would be really helpful.

You: Sure, that's no problem. I'll get that out to you today/tomorrow.

Example Letters (We've Changed the Names)

Letter One

Roger Moore
Universal Exports
Admiralty Arch
Whitehall

Good morning, Roger

I rang. We talked. I asked if I could pop in and see you. You said, "Send me some info in the post", so here it is.

I'm a former lawyer, who turned away from the 'Dark Side' some years ago but now earns a living, training and coaching, trainees to senior partners in communication skills. Over the past 12 months I've worked with loads of law firms (there's a nice list in the blurb) and have even been lucky enough to have won 'The LETG Trainer of the Year' www.letg.org.uk.

Anyway, of late I have come across the names of a number of large Austrian law firms and heard great things about the kind of work they are doing and their attitude towards training and looking after their people, which is why I thought I'd get in touch with firms such as yourselves and arrange to pop in and have a chat with the person responsible for T&D.

I will give you a ring in a few days time to see how your diary's fixed and see if we might have a chat over a coffee, so I can find out more about what you do and whether what I do might be of any help. In the meantime have a look at the blurb I've sent and see what you think.

Until then, thanks a lot.
Nick Davies

Letter Two

Good morning, Sarah

Here, as promised is some more info about what I do.

I'm afraid that my glossy little brochure detailing all this stuff won't hit the streets until the first week of March but this will certainly give you a feel for what I'm about and the way I deliver training.

Hopefully, we will have arranged to meet up on the 28th by the time you get this but no matter if it's not worked out this time round.

Cheers
Nick

Once You Secure the Meeting

If, after a brief chat with Roger, he agrees to meet you for a coffee, thank him and let him know you'll confirm by email.

You should also send him some more information about what you do in the post in anticipation of your get-together: which you may or may not tell him you're going to send.

Sending information ahead of the meet is always a wise move because then they have a far better impression of what you do and will have given them the opportunity to perhaps think of some questions.

If you wait until you meet before furnishing him with the stuff, then at the end of the appointment he can fall back on the "well, I'll think about it once I've taken a look through your literature".

As you'll have realised, we love sending letters because they are a superb way to CONNECT with people and are so very rarely sent in our age of electronic communication. They can really make an impact, and make you stand out from all your competitors.

EXAMPLE of a letter sent confirming a get-together just arranged over the phone:

> Hello Carole
>
> It was lovely to talk to you a moment ago and great that we were able to fix up a time to meet.
>
> Before we get together on the 22nd, I thought it might be helpful if I sent you some info about the sort of thing I do; so here it is.
>
> There is even a photo of me on the inside front cover of my brochure (which might make you think twice before eating before seeing me: I would hate to be responsible for a bout of nausea).
>
> Anyway, see you at 4 on the Thursday.
>
> Regards
> Nick

Voicemail: Talking to a Machine

If you fail to get through to either Roger or his P.A. then chances are you will at least be able to leave a message on his voicemail, which will be along something along the lines of:

> Good afternoon Roger, my name's Nick Davies. I'm a former lawyer but now spend my time training and coaching lawyers at all levels in a variety of communication skills, I do work for firms such X and Y but don't do anything for you. I'd like to pop in, find out more about the firm, and what you do and see whether what I do might be of use and wondered if you were free on either the 4th or 5th?
>
> I'll put some info in the post and give you a ring in a week or so to see which day suits you best. In the meantime, if you want to ring me back, then you can get me on 07777 747 815.

Then send him an amended version of the letter reproduced above.

Here's one Nick sent:

Example One

> Hello Michelle
>
> I left a message on your voice mail to let you know I'd be sending some information about the training I provide: well here it is.
>
> I deliver training to a wide variety of organisations but my background in law and legal recruitment means I spend an awful lot of time helping lawyers polish up their communication skills – whether that be in delivering seminars, pitching for business or networking.
>
> I'm visiting a number of firms in the North of England over the next few months, Dickinson Dees, Watson Burton, Robert Muckle and McKeags to introduce myself, find out how they go about training and see whether what I do might be of help to them now or in the future.
>
> I'd really like to pop in and have a chat with you whilst on my travels and so will give you a ring in a couple of weeks to see if we might put something in the diary.
>
> Regards
> Nick

- Opening line: A friendly greeting.
- Paragraph One: Doing what he said he was going to do (trustworthy).
- Paragraph Two: What he does and has experience in their sector (credibility).
- Paragraph three: Look who else he is going to see (he knows his market (credibility) and doesn't want to miss out.
- Last Paragraph: Telling her what he's going to do and when he's going to do it (keeping control and setting up the FOLLOW-UP?)

The last paragraph is crucial!

We have already mentioned FOLLOWING UP is something that happens at every stage of the process: TARGET, CONNECT, MEET and ASK, the thing that envelops everything we do and you should too!

Here is a good example of it at the foot of this letter. And as you will see, in virtually every other letter or email we ever send.

Never, ever, finish a letter off with: 'In the meantime, if there is anything else I can help you with please don't hesitate to call'.

We've little doubt that over the years, you've received very many letters with this as the concluding sentence. How many times have you rung or emailed the sender? Our point exactly!

Good salespeople hate, just hate, handing control over of the process. They detest the uncertainty it brings, so they make sure that they are in the driving seat.

Nick has told Michelle what he's going to do and when he's going to do it: they both know what's going to happen next.

This is a point we shall be returning to but flag it up here because of its importance.

Example Two

> Good morning, Emma
>
> I'm Nick – the guy who left a voicemail for you yesterday.
>
> Thought some info about me and what I do might be handy, so you'll find a brochure plus copies of the learning materials from my selling course 'Beyond the Business Card' and networking course.
>
> Be great to meet up over a coffee but I appreciate it's short notice so no worries.
>
> I'll not bother you again but may drop you a line in six months to see whether my timing is any better – although you will probably be right in the middle of your move by then.*
>
> Thanks a lot
> Nick

*Whilst chatting with the receptionist she mentioned that the firm was relocating

No Voicemail: Nothing and No One to Talk To

If this is the case, refer to the examples of letters and emails we've given you.

The 'nothing to lose' approach.

There may be occasions when you just think, 'Stuff it, I'm going to get in touch with this person and see what happens. I have nothing to lose'.

This might be when you have no connection with the firm in question and no real prospect of being referred to them or introduced to them by any of your existing contacts, or when, as was the case in the first example I've given when you stumble across an article about an organisation and think that you'd like to go and see them because what they're doing sounds interesting or just appeals.

Here are two examples of when Nick did just that.

From: Nick Davies

To: Lisa

Subject: May the 19th

Hello Lisa

I was rooting through my box of articles and clippings, looking for inspiration for an hour-long presentation I am delivering to 250 senior managers at Aberdeen City Council, when I came across an article from 'The Lawyer' dated the 19th of May 2003, which featured your then-spanking new venture.

I'd kept it because I remember thinking at the time, 'what a bunch of truly commercially focused, entrepreneurial lawyers – good on 'em!' So when I Googled the name of your firm and discovered that you were still thriving, I thought I'd get in touch.

Do you ever see visitors? If you do, I'd like to pop in and see you (I'll bring the coffee and sticky buns) and find out more about what you do and whether what I do might be of help. As to what I do: take a look at www.reallygreattraining.co.uk and have a gander at my biog, which I've attached.

Bye
Nick

I am not going to go through each paragraph again because you should be able to see exactly what I'm doing by now.

Below is her reply.

From: Lisa McDonald

Date: Mon, 16 Jun

Subject: RE: May the 19th 2003

Nick, we do occasionally allow visitors through the door, yes – particularly if they bear gifts of a sticky bun nature. I am assuming, though, that you weren't going to make a special visit from Scotland just to see us! Let me know when you are next planning a trip to London so that we can arrange a suitable time.

Regards
Lisa

My reply,

From: Nick Davies

Sent: 17 June

To: Lisa McDonald

Subject: Re: May the 19th 2003

Special though I'm sure you most undoubtedly are, you are correct in your assumption that I had not intended to travel to London simply to see you all.

The nature of my work means that I'm in your neck of the woods an awful lot of the time. (I have an Oyster card for goodness sake: surely the only one in Edinburgh?)

Anyway, the next time I'm there and have time would be after 5 on the 15th or 16th of July or between 2.30 and 3.30 on the 17th or morning of the 18th.

Let me know how you're fixed and what's best for you Lisa and we'll set something up.

What sort of buns would people like best?

Nick

Her response,

Well, let's make it after 5 on 16th July then. You really don't need to bring any cakes! We'll see you then.

Regards
Lisa

What Happened

Nick and Lisa met. There was nothing he could help them with and they agreed to keep in touch.

In August 2010, Lisa contacted him. Nick ended up delivering a day's worth of training for the partnership, securing and subsequently securing work for two friends of his, both of whom were fellow consultants/trainers and a referral for business to a client of his in a different sector.

Happy days!

Here's another example:

> Good afternoon, Geoff
>
> I was happily minding my own business doing a load of training for all the partners at BLP a couple of months ago, when a bloke called John Smith came up to me, told some story about flogging his house to a Paul Scholes and then said, "Next time you're in town I'll take you for a spot of lunch".
>
> So a few weeks later we do lunch and he says – as I have a mouthful of what he assures me is, "the most expensive sandwich in London" – that I should meet up with you cos, and I quote, "John at Zorin Partners would love the kind of stuff that you've done for us and you'd get on like a house on fire". He then proceeds to write your email address on my napkin and as he hands it to me, adds, "Oh and mention Sarah cos she'd be interested in what you do as well".
>
> So that is why I've got in touch with Geoff. And whilst John suns himself on a boat off the coast of Majorca with his wife, the kids, the best client and the best client mistress (you just could not make it up) I wonder if, when you are next in London, I might buy you a coffee and see if what he says is true.
>
> Cheers
> Nick

That's the transcript of an email Nick sent to the managing partner of one of Europe's largest professional services firms: Cold! (The names have been changed to protect the innocent.)

We wish to draw your attention to a couple of points regarding this email:

Point one

DO NOT WRITE TO ANYONE YOU WISH TO DO BUSINESS WITH, LIKE THIS unless you are happy to take the risk, which all depends on the circumstances and relationships you have.

Point Two

Whilst we have included this email under the chapter 'Cold Calling', you'll notice it's not entirely chilly: more sort of tepid in that although Geoff has no idea of who Nick is, he does have a relationship with John, which is a connection.

Indeed, it is this connection that gave Nick the confidence to send such a confident email. John is a straight-talking bloke who calls a 'spade' a 'bloody shovel'. He and Nick get on well and talking in much the same way and adopt a similar style when talking to people.

John is mates with Geoff, so Nick figured that if John and he could talk to each other in such terms, he'd be reasonably safe in assuming that Geoff would talk in a similar style. (A risk, but a calculated one.)

Point Three

How many emails do you think the CEO of one of Europe's largest professional services firms receives in a day? 200? 400? It's got to be a lot hasn't it – a serious amount!

So when Nick's email lands inbox and he opens it, it has to do the equivalent of reaching out of the screen and grabbing his throat and shouting 'HELLO! LOOK AT ME!'

Point Four

What has he got to lose: Nothing, he didn't do business with this organisation. Nick have never met this bloke and he knows nothing of him or what he does do. So, it's got to be worth a shot hasn't it?

The third point is an important one and, as with a number of other points throughout this book, we make no apology for repeating.

You'll have noticed, not just with this email but in our letters we don't contact people like other salespeople do.

Our style is a bit different and that's because we want to be noticed. In fact, we HAVE to be noticed. What we write, and how we sound, must stand out from all the other communications our prospects receive.

Learning and development managers in large law firms get contacted between 10 and 12 training providers A DAY! 'YES', A DAY! And the vast majority of these contacts, whether they are emailed or arrive by post are never read and deleted. We want to make sure ours aren't and, would strongly suggest, you don't want yours to follow the same fate either!

Sending bland, anonymous, standard letters and emails is a waste of time.

So, what happened once he received the email?

His training and development director got in touch and suggested he and Nick meet.

That's all Nick wanted: a meeting.

They met, got on well and Nick was subsequently invited to pitch for some work.

He didn't end up getting the work (you win some, you lose some). However, when she sent the email telling him he'd been unsuccessful, after expressing his disappointment, he let her know that he'd be in touch nine months later to see where she was up to and whether there was anything else he could help with.

(FOLLOW UP – tell them what you are going to do next and when – even when you don't win the work!)

Even when you get rejected you must always leave the 'door open' because a 'No' now, doesn't mean never. People and circumstances change.

Summary

We have devoted a number of pages to CONNECTING with potential clients and used going in cold as an example.

Depending on where you find yourself with either a hot, warm or tepid contact, you will probably find some of the steps outlined are handy in how to CONNECT with the person you're after.

Some of you will never need to cold call and you should be grateful for that because going in cold is certainly the trickiest way of generating sales. It's just so much easier to sell more stuff to existing clients or tackle those who can be introduced to you by someone else.

Still, there will be some of you that do have to do it and some of you who are just plane odd, like Nick, who do it, just for the thrill of it!

It's now time to look at the most popular business activity; the one that most non-sales people turn to first because it appears much easier than phoning people up. We refer, of course to 'networking'.

The great thing about networking is that it allows you the opportunity to CONNECT and MEET at the same time.

Note

1 For a superb commentary on making such a connection in a pitch situation, we would heartily recommend chapter Four of Jon Steel's book, 'Perfect Pitch'.

Chapter 4

Networking

CONNECT and MEET (Stages Two and Three)

Prior to kicking off, we want to illustrate where networking comes in the whole client/provider/supplier relationship process.

BOND
TRUST
RESPECT
ACCEPTANCE
UNDERSTANDING
ACKNOWLEDGEMENT

When you are out and about developing business, this is the process which you are moving the relationship through: from the bottom to top. Let us explain each step.

Acknowledgement

It is possible to acknowledge someone's existence without having met them. A cold call reveals the name of the contact with whom you need to connect. You come across them on LinkedIn or their organisation's website? You may simply read their name on a delegate list.

Understanding

As with the above, it is quite possible to gain an understanding of what your potential target client does by a look at their profile on LinkedIn or website.

Clearly, when you meet someone at an event and start chatting, you quickly discover what they do for a living and where they work.

Acceptance

At this stage of the relationship, your prospect acceptance they may have a need for the services you provide.

DOI: 10.4324/9781003602422-4

Whilst it is possible for them to do this without having necessarily met you, it's more likely they will have done so in order to fully accept the usefulness of your service.

Respect

If your contact/potential client subsequently asks you for some advice or help on a matter they currently face, to which you provide, timely, relevant and helpful suggestions, then you'll have earned their respect.

Trust

As time goes by and you do more coaching and consulting for them, introducing them to models, which are working, you arrive at a point where trust has been established.

Bond

A bond is forged between you and your client, such that if they move on from their current position and on to a different organisation, they 'take you with them'.

You have a deep understanding of how they 'tick' and like to work and vice versa.

Three points to consider:

Point One

It can take a hell of a long time. Moving through this process to a point where you even do business together, let alone forge a bond can take years and may have meant meeting with a number of people within the organisation.

This is another reason you must target your networking activity and ask for work and referrals from those you know.

If you can attend an event where more people from your target market will be, that's worth going to; even better if one of your contacts can facilitate an introduction.

Similarly, when meeting up for catch-up coffees with existing contacts, aside from asking them whether there is anything else you can help them with, also ask who else they think it would be worth seeing!

Once you have a connection or have done some work for a large organisation you need to be mining it for everything it's worth!

The caveat or warning to this is DO NOT PUT ALL YOUR EGGS IN ONE BASKET! Tempting though it would be to secure that one big, fat, beautiful cash cow, all that needs to happen for your business to go belly up is for a new purchasing manager to come along and tell you they have changed supplier because 'they want to freshen things up' a little!

NEVER, EVER, EVER, stop developing business. EVER

Point Two

Recognise the fact you are going to meet many people in the course of developing business; who you get on with, understand what you do and accept that what you offer could be of benefit to them but the relationship does not move to the respective stage because they don't buy from you.

Why? They already have a relationship with a consultant or coach.

And here's the thing; if they are happy with them, why on earth would they change?

However, nothing lasts forever and relationships do change. Suppliers and purchasers move to other jobs, and comprehensive supplier reviews are conducted. Coaches get sloppy, take business for granted, cut corners, cock up or simply take their eye off the ball.

When you meet someone who is happy with their current supplier, ask them if it is ever reviewed. Otherwise, keep their details/connected on LinkedIn and drop them a line every six months so you keep up to date with what's going on and so you remain in their consciousness.

Final Point

Relax! Make it easy for yourself. Far too many people put themselves under pressure when they go to networking events, as though they MUST meet someone who will end up being a client. Nonsense! You'll meet loads of really interesting people whilst networking but very few will end up being clients.

Stage Two: CONNECT

What Sorts of Networking?

When most people think about networking they conjure up a room full of strangers, with name badges on, clutching glasses of Pinot, whilst balancing a plate of nibbles, desperately worried about breaking into a group of people and indulging in interesting conversation: anxious they appear both interested and interesting.

We would also include in networking, those conversations you may strike up with complete strangers on the train, plane or waiting room.

LinkedIn

Think of LinkedIn as a networking event, which is open 24 hours a day, 7 days a week and 365 days a year.

When you're asleep, people can approach you, introduce themselves and request to connect.

LinkedIn can be a very useful tool in your business and help you accomplish some useful things:

- Keep in touch
- Message
- Learn when people move jobs/get promoted
- Wish them a happy anniversary or birthday
- Comment when they attend events
- Acknowledge when they win awards
- Share posts and news with your network
- Prospect
- Raising your profile
- Compile target lists

Below are the four Ps, aimed and helping you get the most from this powerful platform.

We'd like to thank the wonderful Jim Meldrum for permission to reproduce his process here. For more details about the help Jim can provide go to www.nustrategy.co.uk.

Social Selling Index

Take a look at this link…

https://www.linkedin.com/sales/ssi

Now you know what your social selling index is, and how it compares to others in your sector and networking, and how it's arrived at.

Keep an eye on this as you begin 'doing' LinkedIn and watch it rise!

- PROFILE
- PROCESS
- PROSPECT and
- POST

PROFILE

Your profile is your shop window, make sure your talents and skills are displayed properly.

Names: Use the name by which you are known! Nick's full name is 'Nicholas'. However, He is known as 'Nick', which is why he listed under the latter. People wouldn't find him as easily, if at all if he was listed under 'Nicholas'.

You need a professional shot photograph of you. NOT you and your dog, daughter, best mate, life partner. You wouldn't have them stood next to you at a networking event nor named on your business card!

Your profile banner should be equally professional – your logo, brand colours, etc. Also, use it to provide contact information.

In the space for text, be sure to detail what it is you help people with, rather than your qualifications.

In the 'About' section of your profile, use the full allocation of characters allowed. The information here is searchable so make sure it contains all the skills and talents you offer.

'Endorsements' and 'Recommendations' Whilst it's nice to receive endorsements, they count for nothing by the LinkedIn algorithm. If people give you them, great and see if they are happy to put a finger to the keyboard and leave you a recommendation, to which weight IS attached!

If someone thanks you for doing a good job, be in the habit of asking if they'd be happy to leave a recommendation, because 'it would be really very helpful'.

PROCESS

Both Jim Meldrum and we suggest you 'do' LinkedIn first thing, before you've even opened your inbox.

Whilst the app is very useful for when you are out and about, particularly at networking events when you can connect with people there and then, the fact is, the desktop version has far more functionality.

Here's the sequence we recommend...

Home – take a look here at what's been going on in your network, with people and organisations you follow. This is where you'll see people attending conferences, award ceremonies, trips away, off-site, etc.

Comment, like or acknowledge the ones you like and share them. Do you think your connections would like to see it?

However, do not do a LAZY share! Add something to it – your comments and thoughts. Acknowledge them in your 'share' and name anyone within your network you think who'd be particularly interested.

Spend no more than a couple of minutes scrolling through your 'home' because it's all too easy to end up reading and reading, post after post!

My Network Click here and then on to 'connections', where those who have accepted your connection requests will appear. Thank them for their connection and ask them how they're doing/how is their business doing.

What you are trying to do is get a conversation going. Relax if it doesn't. It's no big deal. However, if you find yourself exchanging a few messages, maybe suggest moving things on to a Zoom or Teams call, or even better, an in-person chat.

Messaging This icon is your next stop and where people have messaged you.

Reply as necessary and appropriate with an eye to possibly getting a 'conversation' going.

Notifications Notifications are always busiest at the start of the week because it's here where people let others know they have either been promoted, started a new job/role or taken on another role, to run alongside their current one.

Not only is it useful to keep up to date with what your contacts are up to and where, but it also opens up possibly two opportunities...

1. Someone has filled or is going to fill their former role, with whom you can now endeavour to cultivate a relationship.
2. Chances are they have moved to an organisation with which you do not currently count as a client, and, assuming, your relationship is strong enough, could now get you into that organisation.

If, when registering on the platform, people have given their date of birth, it's under 'notifications' where you'll see when people are celebrating and can wish them a very Happy Birthday.

LinkedIn conveniently provides the users with default 'congrats on the new rob/promotion' and 'Happy Birthday!'

DO NOT be tempted to use these!

Here is an opportunity to type a tailored message, so you stand out from all the other 'cookie cutter' platitudes!

You needn't compose a different one for each person, simply cut and paste your bespoke comment.

One of Nick's favoured birthday messages goes...

> 'Happy Birthday Claire!
> I hope you enjoy a thoroughly indulgent day?! Jelly and cake all round!'

PROSPECT

LinkedIn is a great way to target, very precisely, those with whom you wish to build a relationship AND there are no secretaries, receptionists or PAs getting in the way.

You can create your own search lists, using the level of connection, sector, organisation, geographical area and role, to make sure you are targeting precisely the right people.

At the time of writing, LinkedIn will allow you to send a limited number of connection requests with messages if you are not paying for the 'premium' service.

Our suggestion is to therefore miss out on messages completely and just send a request: you will be amazed how many people will accept and once they have, you are then free to message them.

POST

Posting is important, but not all posts are treated equally. You need to know what LinkedIn likes and doesn't like!

Most people are under the impression when they post, it will be seen by everyone in their network – their 'first' level connections.

This is not the case! LinkedIn's algorithm sends it to only 10% of them, before monitoring interaction with it – likes, comments, shares, re-posts, etc., – for a period of somewhere between 60 and 120 minutes.

If, after such time, your post has had little engagement, it is put in LinkedIn's giant rubbish bin, as though no one had seen it! It will remain in your profile as something you contributed but the sad fact is, hardly anyone saw it.

If, however, after the 'golden' period has elapsed, and it is gaining traction, it will be sent to 50% of your contacts, and the same process will be repeated.

LinkedIn is only interested in information which is causing 'dwell time' – what's keeping people looking at our platform?! If your stuff isn't, it gets binned!

Between 60 and 120 minutes elapse again and it is still attracting 'likes', 'shares', 'comments', etc., it is then sent to the remainder of your first-level contacts.

Only after that, and assuming it's still attracting 'dwell time', it will be sent out to the wider LinkedIn community.

What Sorts of Posts?

- Education – share your knowledge
- Inspiration – share success stories
- Information – 'Attend our event!'
- Entertainment – the Funny Fail (attract MOST attention)

The posts which attract the most attention are those featuring people's faces. We are naturally drawn to others. It's human nature. If you can post an image with lots of people, so much the better. It might be a group of you attending an away day, picking up an award on stage or fellow delegates attending a conference. These initiate dwell time because people are looking for themselves and friends and colleagues are looking for them, 'Oh, that's the conference/awards Tammy was at. Oh, look! I've found her!'

A final note regarding posting...

If you are wondering, 'Should I post this?' The answer is probably NO!

Whilst networking using a sophisticated platform like LinkedIn is valuable, it should never be a substitute for face-to-face networking.

Establishing trust is much harder and even when it is, it is much more fragile. In-person relationships are far more stable and secure.

Do not be fooled into thinking because you are connected to perhaps tens or even hundreds of people, you have a relationship with them, let alone one that would lead to business. In order to achieve that, you have to go and see them.

In the Summer of 2009, Harvard Business Review Analytical Services conducted a survey of 2,211 business people across, the UK, the US, France and Germany to examine how valuable doing business face-to-face was compared to using the growing range of hi-tech alternatives. The results of which are illuminating.

95% of business people said that face-to-face meetings were the key to success in building long-term relationships. 83% said that personal relationships were impossible without face-to-face meetings and 81% said that face-to-face meetings improve productivity and results.

Stage Three: MEET?

The 'Networking Event'

Speaking: better than working a room

Before we get into the whole 'working a room' lark, it's important to point out that which should be obvious...

Rather than attending an event and having to establish credibility and trust with a whole host of people, why not dazzle the entire room in one go by getting up and speaking at it!

A story from the Nick 'story locker'

Nick had reached firm 16 on his top 20 list. He contacted the guy who headed up the training and development team and got an appointment to see him for a coffee.

During their conversation, the prospect asked me if I'd heard of the LETG (The Legal Education and Training Group). I hadn't.

He went on to explain that it was an association made up of the heads of training and development at the principal law firms in the country.

The conversation then continued thus:

Nick: When is your annual conference?
Him: November.

(*The conversation took place in March*)

Nick: I'd really like to speak at that. How can I go about making that happen?

Him: Mm, that might be a possibility. Leave it with me and I'll have a word with a few people.

Result – Nick spoke at that conference. Although not one of the main speakers; he was asked to run one of four 'break-out' sessions, which delegates could opt to attend and was persuaded to deliver a bit of an impromptu after-lunch speech for the delegates.

This was a huge profile raiser for Nick, right in front of his target market and led directly to some valuable paid work and relationships, which remain important today.

If you are not a confident speaker, go and get some coaching (we can teach you!) and start speaking. It'll set you apart from your competitors, ensure you are remembered by your target audience and what's more you'll gain the trust and credibility essential for effective influence and persuasion.

Attend the Right Events

When you first embark on your journey to becoming a well-remunerated coach and consultant, the temptation is to join generic networking groups. The kind where you turn up every week, have to do a little speech about what your business does and furnish another member with the name of a lead.

Whilst these are lovely social get-togethers filled with bonhomie, they tend to be filled by people just starting up their own business all of whom share one thing in common – they haven't got any money.

It's true, they probably know people who could benefit from your services but why not find out which events they attend and attend them?!

You do not have the luxury of wasting your time – especially in the early days of developing your business – of attending the wrong events! If you're unsure which events to attend, just ask yourself whether the people there are in your HOT, WARM, TEPID or COLD market.

Go to events where you know there are going to be people from the sectors you want to get into or sell to already. The term used in the first *Top Gun* film was 'a target-rich environment'.

Prior to the Event

Contact the organiser and ask them for a delegate list so you can see whether the people from the sectors you're interested in are attending. If they say they can't give out a delegates list because of data protection, thank them for their time and then contact someone else involved in organising the event and see if you have better luck.

Assuming you get hold of a list, take a look at it and find the names of anyone you know already who's going. Contact them and check if they still intend to be there. Sending a connection request via LinkedIn is useful here too, because you can tell them you are attending the same event as them and are hoping to meet.

This is a good thing to do because there is nothing worse than walking into a networking event, not knowing anyone and then having to strike up a conversation with strangers. Whilst it's dumb to spend all evening chatting to someone you know already, knowing there will be someone there you can have as your first point of contact can be reassuring.

Another advantage of hooking up with this person is they may be able to introduce you to people they know but you don't. Either way, going to a networking event and talking all evening with someone you know already is a complete waste of time.

At the Event

Turn up looking the part.

Most people judge other people by their appearance. If you're one of those people who doesn't then be aware that the rest of us do: it's all we have to go on.

The Three Stages of Intimacy

Research done by Desmond Morris, the anthropologist and author of the famous 70s book, 'The Naked Ape', discovered when two human beings meet, they move through the following stages of body language...

- Eye to body
- Eye to eye
- Hand to hand

Eye to Body

What we do here, at a very basic level, in the limbic part of our brain is ask 'friend or foe'. Is this someone it's safe to approach or should they be avoided?

It might sound brutal but it's hardwired into us and means how you appear matters.

Whether we like it or not, we are perhaps not judged by our appearance but most certainly an assessment is made.

A general rule of thumb is to look a little smarter than you think you should. Arrive too scruffy and it's difficult to dress things up, however, arrive too smart and simply removing your tie or jacket or undoing a top button can create a more relaxed appearance.

When you arrive, or perhaps just before, pop into a loo, wash your hands, check your flies/buttons, check your teeth for spinach, reapply lippy, wipe over your shoes to make sure they're clean and make sure you're 'tucked in'.

This all assumes that what you are wearing is clean, laundered, ironed and fits and that basic personal hygiene issues are attended to – clean nails, washed and tidy hair, sufficient deodorant, clean teeth, etc.

Once again, it's about establishing trust and credibility. And let's be honest, if you can't dress yourself properly then you are making it difficult for yourself to establish either of these, particularly the latter.

Eye to Eye

We tend not to trust people who don't look us in the eye; we regard them as 'shifty'. Equally, you don't want to be staring at people, so look into their eyes and around their face. The vast majority of us look at a person's mouth when they are talking to us, which is fine, just don't neglect the eyes. And for goodness sake, don't look over someone's shoulder as they are speaking to you: it's really off-putting.

Hand to Hand

We don't 'do' touching in our society. Walk down a busy high street or get on public transport and see how much effort we go into avoiding touching each other. In such a culture, the handshake takes on a whole new significance.

Getting hold of another person's hand is a pretty intimate thing to do, so make sure your handshake is a decent one – dry, firm and brief. So much information is conveyed in that handshake.

Dry – sweaty hands are a big 'NO'! Before you go into a meeting, have an interview or embark on some networking, go and wash your hands always!

Firm – not bone crunching but neither light nor weak. Like Goldilocks's porridge, it should be 'just right'.

Well, credibility is something that is established right from the start of a relationship; right from that very first encounter: A firm handshake, whilst looking someone in the eye, introducing yourself and saying, "Very pleased to meet you". Is a superb way of establishing your credibility and parity with them, right from the off.

The reason the handshake is so important is down to a wonderful chemical… Oxytocin.

Oxytocin is a neurotransmitter, which has two powerful effects:

It bonds us – we feel more connected to the other person.

It relaxes us.

The power of the handshake cannot be underestimated. Make sure you start every relationship with it!

Who Do You Talk To?

Well, if you have arrived with someone, then start with them (it'd be rude not to.)

If, having checked the delegate list, you wish to talk to somebody in particular, whilst you're at the registration point, ask the organisers whether that person has arrived and, if so, if they can point them out.

Nick has been on the receiving end of this and it's quite flattering when someone you don't know approaches you and says, "Hi, you must be Nick Davies, my name is Max Kalber, I hope you don't mind me introducing myself but I really wanted to meet you and have a chat".

What's more, it delays the point at which you have to look around the room for someone to talk to and that can only be a good thing because, if you're anything like Nick, that's always the awkward bit.

In fact, let's deal with that right now.

Getting Conversations Going

OK, you have arrived at registration and pinned your badge on.

Go to the area where the drinks are. Invariably this is tea or coffee. Pour yourself a cup. Nine times out of ten, another delegate will approach the table in anticipation of pouring themselves a drink once you've done. Look towards them and ask, "Are you having coffee?" If they answer "yes", give them the one you've just poured. Or, if they've poured theirs already and are waiting for you to finish with the milk, ask them if they'd like milk. If "yes", pour it for them.

This works with any liquid!

We use this natural icebreaker all the time because we're not keen on walking up to strangers either and the 'coffee routine' is relaxed, perfectly natural and really easy to do, not to mention very effective.

When Nick was director of the recruitment firm he did this, got talking to the person concerned, who turned out to be a fantastic recruitment consultant with a rival agency, and they ended up working for us and bringing in loads of cash – all from a simple "would you like coffee?"

It also works because it brings in a little bit of psychology surrounding 'reciprocity'. If you give another person something for free, without being asked, they feel terribly obliged to give you something in return and in this scenario, it's time.

Imagine if you arrived at the drinks table at a networking event, were offered a cup of coffee someone had poured for themselves and you just said "thanks" and walked away.

How rude!

A bit about food and remembering names.

Food

This is another subject that can create anxiety.

"It's so awkward when you have a glass in one hand and a plate of food in the other and you're attempting to have a conversation with someone. What on earth do you do? I always feel so self-conscious".

Put the plate down and finish what's in your mouth.

Remembering Names

First thing: you don't forget the names of people you meet. It's simply you don't hear them in the first place.

When two people meet for the first time and go through those initial three steps of body language outlined earlier – eye to body, eye to eye and then hand to hand.

During this process, there is what is referred to as 'visual noise'. So when the person tells you their name, you're almost deaf to it, which explains why after only a few seconds you are looking at them and thinking, 'I have absolutely no idea what you are called!'

Now, if you're at an event where people are wearing name badges then this is not too much of a problem, other than having to contort yourself to read it clearly.

Once you know this visual noise business is happening, what do you do the next time someone introduces themselves to you or you are introduced to them, you repeat their name as soon as they have said it.

Me: Hi, my name's Nick.
Pearce: Hi, I'm Pearce.
Me: Hi Pearce, pleased to meet you.

And then you use their name two or three times during the first couple of minutes and in that way you 'cement' it in your memory.

If you fail to do this, then you can always ask them to repeat it:

"Do you know, I'm terrible at names, what's yours again, I didn't quite catch it I'm afraid".

You have had someone ask you that before haven't you? How did you feel? Offended? Cut to the quick? Of course not! And neither will be anyone that you have to ask. In fact I would suggest that asking the person to repeat their name, sends a very strong signal telling them their name is so important to you, you have asked them again.

Awkward and seemingly unpronounceable names

Look, don't struggle when you meet someone with an unusual name and certainly don't spend time talking to them without using their name. It's obvious to both parties when this is happening and really awkward if someone joins the conversation and looks to you for an introduction and you have no idea what to say.

If someone with an unusual name introduces themselves and you don't get the pronunciation straight off, ask them to pronounce it again. They won't mind. They are used to people struggling with their name: they've experienced it all their life!

What we have found is they are more than happy to help you get the pronunciation right and are chuffed, you've been one of the few people to ever take the time to get it right: most people just mumble on!

Moving in and Moving on

Moving In

Ok, so you've no one to talk to when walking into the event and no one able to introduce you to someone and no opportunity has arisen at the drinks table?

First, you need to make an assessment of the room.

There may be a couple of large groups of individuals gathered together. There are a number of smaller groups, comprising three or four people. Then they are a number of 'couples' and of course, finally, people, like you, who are on their own.

Groups of Four or More

Hard to break into don't bother: it's too difficult and too awkward. However, if it's your only choice, approach the group so you are facing the person speaking and make eye contact with them so they know you are entering and acknowledge you.

Groups of Three or Four

Easier than the big groups but you still need to approach with caution.

The first thing to do is size these groups up. If from the body language and position of each person or from their conversation – assuming you can hear it – it would appear that they are work colleagues and deep in conversation about issues in their office, then leave them to it.

Even if these people are not from the same firm, they may be continuing a conversation that began in the taxi on the way to the event. Again, leave them to it.

On the other hand, if you get the feeling they are not colleagues and their body language suggests this is a relaxed, informal group, approach them and ask if you can join them.

This does rely on you being assertive and probably taking a deep breath before making a move but if the alternative is standing on your own all evening it's got to be preferable!

Two People

People in twos are easier to approach, although once again you must make an assessment based on their body language and position relative to one another.

If they are close and there's touching then it's perhaps prudent to leave them to it. Otherwise, twos are often, at least subconsciously, looking for a third person to join them and you can clearly see this in the way they are standing relative to each other.

Very often you'll see two people who are standing at 'ten to two' next to each other, as though waiting for someone to complete the triumvirate. Be aware of this – you'll be amazed at how many times you witness it. It's an invitation for someone to join them, so accept it.

People Alone

People alone are the easiest to talk to. They are in exactly the same boat as you. They feel awkward and anxious about making an approach.

To sum up: The coffee/tea ploy works a treat. If that's not viable go and speak to someone who's on their own.

That's 'moving in' done so what about moving on?

Moving On

You've been chatting to someone for a while and feel the conversation has run its course. You may want to get an opportunity to meet this person again and chat further about matters that have arisen or in areas you have in common business-wise but we will talk about the follow-up meeting later. For now, we just want to give you some tips about moving on.

First of all DO NOT fall back on the old, "Well if you'll excuse me I need to go and freshen up my drink". Or "if you'll excuse me I just need to pop to the loo".

The problem with both these is the person with whom you are conversing may decide they need to do the same and end up following you.

Whilst someone accompanying you to the drinks area might be a bit of a pain when you want to get away from them, it's not half as awkward as them following you to the bathroom!

There are a couple of options here:

Moving On – Tip Number One

"Well Tim, it's been lovely to chat to you this evening and hear about your business and the stuff that's going on, however, there are a few other people I'd like to catch up with whilst I'm here, so if you'll excuse me I'll go and seek them out".

This is assertive, honest and unambiguous.

There are people who feel this is a little bit mean because it does result in leaving the other person to fend for themselves as it were. However, Tim's a grown-up. He's been to networking events before and understands you aren't there to spend the next two hours with him.

Moving On – Tip Number Two (This Is the Best One)

Rather than leave people on their own ask if they know 'Joanne' or 'Dave' or one of any number of people with whom you might already know at the event.

You Nick, have you had the pleasure of meeting Joanne from KPMG yet?
Me: No, I can't say I have.
You: Well let me introduce you to her. She's just over there.

Then guide me across to where Joanne is standing talking, furnishing me with a bit of information about how you know her, her role and any personal info you might be aware of … 'She is a big dog lover', 'She's mad on F1 racing' and 'She's just come back from holidaying in Costa Rica'.

He'd move over to where Joanne was.

You: Hi Jo, sorry to interrupt but there's someone I'd really like you to meet. Nick, Joanne, Joanne, Nick Davies from really great training

"Nick's originally from Manchester/is a big footie fan/does a bit of Stand Up Comedy/has a passion for shoes!" used to run a catering business.

Once the introductions are complete, bid us goodbye and move on.

Introducing someone to another contact is lovely for everyone concerned.

It's good for you because you can move on to the next person in the knowledge you've not left your current contact having to find someone else.

It works for your contact because they are not in the awkward position of having to chat with a stranger and don't feel abandoned.

It works for the person to whom you have introduced your contact because they have now met someone new without having to go and talk to a stranger or break into a group.

And here's another thing. You and your contact might have enjoyed a good chat and got on well, but there has been no business connection.

Just because this encounter is not going to lead to anything it doesn't necessarily follow the same will be the case between them and another person. They could get on like a house on fire and end up having a very profitable business relationship.

In the course of trying to find the ideal business connection, you will meet a lot of people you like, get on with and have a laugh with; it doesn't necessarily mean you want to take it further or that just because they aren't the 'right one' for you, that they aren't absolutely 'right' for someone else.

Once again, the message surrounding networking has to be RELAX – it's about chatting to people. If business springs forth from it, great, if it doesn't, it's not the end of the world.

Everybody who attends a networking event knows the purpose behind it: to make contacts and win potential business. However, they are also about increasing your general knowledge of business, learning more about a particular sector and keeping up to date with the latest developments. Most of the time they're good fun and, on occasion, a marvellous way of feeding yourself on the way home.

An equally important aspect of networking at targeted events is that they allow you to increase your profile.

Standing Out and Being Remembered

One of the single biggest benefits to just networking within the markets you have targeted is that each time you attend a relevant event you raise your profile.

This is why you should always try and speak at events: standing up in front of your target market is the best way to stand out and be remembered.

Either, fortunately or unfortunately, we now live in a society in which standing out and being noticed is increasingly important.

There are so many organisations, people and institutions desperately trying to vie for our attention every day of the week.

LinkedIn, Instagram, X, FaceBook, TikTok, WhatsApp, Text, email, voicemail, etc.: We are bombarded by people and companies trying to draw our attention to something.

It's therefore really quite difficult to stand out and even more important people remember you.

The consultancy and coaching business is awash with providers.

Stage two of the MODEL is 'CONNECT', and that doesn't just mean getting in touch with them, it means making an emotional connection: striking a chord, resonating and appealing to their emotional side.

We don't simply mean at formal networking events but if you are at a dinner or corporate jolly. It's about when you get chatting to someone outside the loo on a crowded train out of Leeds or are whisked through security at Stansted, by a member of the airline you are flying with.

We notice, and remember people who stand out.

There are plenty of ways in which to differentiate yourself and be remembered in your networks...for the RIGHT reasons!

Standing out is about being remembered for your personality, for doing a great job (although we would argue that was a given) for your clothing – maybe you have a reputation for wearing funky shirts, amazing shoes, a pocket square in your jacket, next scarves?

Maybe you are always the life and soul of the party? Perhaps you are the marathon runner in the office, or the sailor or the campanologist (look it up) or maybe you're the only person who ever thanks customers and clients for their business: sending flowers or cards to organisers of events and admin people, working behind the scenes who almost always get overlooked?

A while ago, Nick, as part of his daily LinkedIn 'routine', wished a connection a Happy Birthday.

However, rather than going with the platform's default 'Happy Birthday!' He added, 'I hope you enjoy a thoroughly indulgent day! Jelly and cake all round!'

The recipient of the message replied: "Thanks, Nick. I have had 32 messages wishing me a 'happy birthday'. However, yours was the ONLY one that wasn't the standard one. It really stood out!"

The point is, people notice when you do even just a little bit more and make slightly extra effort than everyone else.

You need a 'story', a few 'highlights', a few little snippets that make you easy to remember – for the right reasons.

The best way to illustrate what we mean is by sharing with you what people remember about Nick.

First of all, he's six feet three inches tall, has a Mancunian accent and wears glasses, physical attributes people recall.

In fact, his accent was commented on fairly recently by a rather well-to-do young lawyer working in London, who was part of a group that he was training.

He came up to Nick during a coffee break and said he thought his accent was probably a really useful thing to have in the job he does.

Nick agreed and wanted to know why he thought it was such an asset.

To which he replied,

"Because everyone else that does training in London and in particular, the City all have the same accent and so yours will really stand out".

And he's bang on and Nick's fully aware of this fact.

Aside from the physical stuff, there's also Nick's work history and his hobbies. He used to sell shoes and still has a real passion for them. He was a lawyer and performed stand-up comedy for ten years and loves funky shirts.

That's it but that'll do! He's happy if that's what people remember him for.

Chances are your clients will be in similar sectors, geographical areas and industries. Such people talk to each other not only at annual conferences, exhibitions and award ceremonies but also via email and phone. They are connected via LinkedIn. They ask each other's advice: "Who do you use for this sort of work?" "We are contemplating using this person for this subject; do you know anything about them?"

If you've done a good job and one of your clients says, "Yeah, we use Tamara O'Connell", to which the other person says, "Oh, now I have heard the name somewhere but have never met her, although I'm sure Sean at Universal Exports was mentioned her a few weeks ago".

Your client might reply:

"Yeah, she's that tall woman from Dublin who used to be an engineer with Aer Lingus. I seem to recall she has a thing about shoes, is a keen golfer and is mad about her 2 Labradoodles!"

"Oh, yes, I know who you mean. I think Holly at Moonraker Inc. has used her recently. Have you got her details?"

These kinds of conversations go on in suppliers networks every day of the week. People in the same positions and same sectors are always sharing information about suppliers.

Make sure people are talking about you and recommending you rather than your competitors! Stand out! Doing a good job is a given so be remembered for other things.

Just turn up.

One of the easiest ways of being remembered and standing apart from your competitors is to turn up.

The virtual meeting has numerous advantages, however, one of them is not establishing and cultivating trust.

The sad fact is that many people cannot be bothered travelling to meet people, preferring the ease of Teams and Zoom.

The fact that you have been prepared to walk, take a train and get in a car clearly demonstrates you are serious about getting to know them and their business. You are, quite literally, prepared to go the extra mile!

In a similar vein is picking up the phone when a potential client emails.

It's tempting to simply email back but telephoning is immediate and a far better way of making an emotional connection with your prospect. It's nice for you both to be able to put a voice to a name.

It also allows scope for some small talk (more about that later).

We've always found if we respond to an email enquiry by phoning the prospect is one surprised and two delighted. Rebecca and Nick have often been told, "Oh, it's so nice to talk to talk to someone on the phone for a change!"

> There is only one thing worse than being talked about, and that is not being talked about.
>
> My biggest mistake, the one for which I can never forgive myself, is that one day I ceased my obsessive pursuit of my own individuality.
>
> Oscar Wilde

Earlier on in the book we showed you examples of the letters and emails Nick has sent to people. They too are intended to make that vital emotional connection with the recipient. Later on, you'll see examples of the different types communication that he's used after having met someone at a networking event. First of all, let's have a look at what you're going to talk about at the event and how you're going to move the conversation along.

Small Talk

As we shake hands and introduce ourselves we begin talking. It's this bit of the encounter we wish to highlight now.

When we meet someone for the first time, we begin to establish a relationship by indulging in an activity known as, 'self disclosure' and we do this via what we all know as 'small talk' or 'chit-chat'.

Those in business often knock such talk as frivolous nonsense. They worry they won't be taken seriously or regarded as professional if they aren't keeping the conversation to matters of business, which is why, all too often, people start up a conversation with something like:

"So, how's business?" Or "What's keeping you awake at night?" "What does the rest of the year/next 2 quarters look like for you and your sector?"

The Topics

Whilst there are undoubtedly variations in which topics are preferred depending on where you are in the world, generally speaking, the following tend to be the principal ones:

- The weather
- Travel (how did you get here today?)
- Holidays
- Sport – football*
- Kids
- Weekend plans/what you did at the weekend

- Pets
- Food

We want to talk about the weather. Well, we would. Wouldn't we? We are British.

There are societies and cultures in which being polite is an overt, active thing.

North America is one such society.

An American you have never met before will be quite happy to walk up to you and introduce himself to you with a hearty handshake and say, "Hi, my name's Hank, I'm from Iowa".

Now, for someone from Great Britain, that's too much information, too soon.

In the UK we can get chatting to someone, talk to them for half an hour before saying, "I'm sorry, I didn't quite catch your name.", in the full knowledge we both know that neither of us has told each other our name.

The reason is that in our society, being polite means not imposing ourselves on others, leaving them to themselves and respecting their privacy, which is why we have, over the years, come up with techniques to initiate conversations that do not make one another other feel uncomfortable, such as making some comment about the weather.

The weather is such a good subject in the UK is, first, that it varies a great deal; second, we all experience it; and third, because it's a great leveller.

No matter how old or young you are, how little or much money you earn or where you were educated or brought up, the weather is something we can all chat about.

For some reason, we are obsessed with finding out how people we meet got 'here' today. We want to know and compare routes, and modes of transport and share travel horror stories with one another.

Of course, if the weather disrupts travel, we Brits are in small-talk heaven!

*I don't know anything about football!

You don't need to know.

A few years ago, Nick got into the back of a taxi in London. After a few minutes of conversation, he asked the driver if he had heard the football scores (it was a Sunday evening), to which he replied, 'I don't know mate, I am not into football".

This was unusual. Most of the time the cabbie supports a team and a conversation naturally follows.

So Nick asked him, "what he was into?"

"Endurance racing", came the reply.

Nick guessed this was ultra-marathons or similar but was quickly corrected and told it referred to motorsport, in particular, LeMans, the annual, 24-hour race, which takes place in that French town.

Whilst Nick had heard of the race, his knowledge was, to say the least, minimal!

Over the following 25 minutes' journey, he learned all about endurance racing and the cabbie's 26-year-old son, 'David' and the journeys and experiences they had shared over the many years they'd been driving to and from the circuit, along with details of the previous team winners, plus all manner of additional facts and stats!

As with all interactions with others – you have two ears and one mouth: use them in those proportions.

When people meet someone who knows very little or nothing regarding a subject about which they are passionate, they love telling them all about it! So let them! You'll learn about the subject and be afforded an insight into what kind of person they are, and what motivates them, which, in turn, will help you remember them and when you do follow up, have something to ask.

With specific regard to football, one only has to make a cursory internet search to find out which teams are playing, in which competitions and any other associated gossip. This will at least enable you to say, "Although football is not my thing, I was reading that...what are your thoughts?"

Remember, whilst at first chat, you may doubt you share little, if anything, in common with the person opposite, it's often the case things come to light, which means you share more than you thought.

Example

Some years ago, Nick arrived at a hotel in Derby, where he'd been booked to talk to 70 trainee lawyers about networking skills.

Before he did his bit, he got chatting with the senior partner of the large national firm with whom these delegates were going to work.

Now this guy was very well-presented, exceptionally well-spoken.

They did the handshake and 'pleased to meet you' bit and fell into easy conversation about 'Casino Royale' (the film had recently been released), the role of Daniel Craig in comparison to previous Bonds, the way the director had interpreted the book, etc.

Nick then made some comments regarding this guy's footwear, which resulted in a conversation about men's shoes, tailoring and suiting.

There was a natural pause in the conversation and Nick remarked that all they'd done for 20 minutes was indulge in small talk.

The senior partner paused for a moment and looked thoughtfully before saying:

> Do you know, I don't think that I've ever won a piece of work based on my technical ability as a lawyer; not one. I've won clients because I play tennis, because I have an interest in men's fashion and because I have a house in the South of France but never solely on my knowledge of the law.

His observation reflects what all those who earn their living in sales can attest to. Customers, and clients, buy things and deal with people they like and we tend to like those who are like us!

Not everyone you meet whilst out and about is going to end up being a client and that's OK. What absolutely, positively and most definitely does matter, however, is that when you part company they come away with a favourable impression of you; as someone whose company they really enjoyed. Not mates for life but have felt that they've met a genuinely nice person who was genuinely interested in what they had to say.

We know that can sound kind of naff 'nice person' but as Sir Digby – now Lord Jones, former chairman of The CBI, said at a speech Nick saw him once deliver; "Contrary to popular belief, genuinely, nice, honest, decent people actually do rather well in business".

Make a Note!

One last thing about small talk: take note of it. Not all of the stuff you've heard and not whilst the person is talking to you. But make sure, that afterwards – maybe whilst sitting in the car just before you leave the venue or on the train home or even the next day in the office – you make a note of the salient points.

The date and place you met them – it's amazing how quickly you'll forget. Along with stuff that's personal to them, such as where they are going on holiday, what football team they support, how many kids they have and their ages, about any big event coming up, such as a wedding, weekend away, what they used to do for a living, where they hail from originally.

Even better, if your organisation has some kind of client relationship system (CRM) then put all you know into that.

All this info is not there in order for you to embark on a campaign of quality stalking but so that in three months, when you look back at your contacts, you'll be better able to remember them and make use of some snippets of information to help the FOLLOW-UP call a whole lot easier: you'll be able to CONNECT with them– as I will illustrate later on.

Moving It on to Business-Talk

You've done what might be referred to as 'social small-talk' but unless you're only at this event for a bit of a social you really need to move on to business.

Following on from the chit-chat, there will normally arrive a point at which one or both parties instinctively feel it's time to move things on a little. There are no hard and fast rules with this – 'just do small talk for 7 minutes and then you must talk business' – so you need to be aware of signals that may indicate it is appropriate to conversationally 'move on'.

Here are some:

- So, Jane, what brings you to this event this afternoon?
- I see from your delegate badge you work for the I.D.A.; what do they do?
- Oh, you normally get off at Bank; is your office far from there? So, what exactly is it that you do?
- You're in the Real Estate team at Linklaters. What exactly does that mean you do there?

All the above are what we might term 'linking' questions. Questions that are great for moving on to work-related stuff. Asking questions is good because as every salesperson knows, being good at selling is not about being able to talk, it's about asking questions, shutting up and listening.

Two reasons for this:

One, it's interesting to learn more about what other people do.

Second, the more you learn about someone's business the easier it is to discover whether the services you offer might be of value to them because if it is, and you get on with them, that's what's going to prompt you to get a business card/LinkedIn connection from them and follow up!

If that's not the case, at least you will have increased your knowledge of business generally and have shared a good old chat with them but probably not felt the need to ask for a business card, put them on your database or invite them to connect on LinkedIn.

Just as there are topics of social small talk, there are topics of business small talk too.

Then each sector has its topics of small talk: local government, construction, defence, law, accountancy, retail and so on.

Each sector then has areas within that, so taking law, for example, these include, construction, employment, real estate plus many more. Sure enough, each one of those has certain subjects and issues that form the topics of conversation.

So if you are targeting the commercial property sector, for example, then you should know what's going on in that field. (No pun intended.) You won't know as much as the surveyors or agents or lawyers but a read through the latest copy of the relevant trade press (probably 'Estates Gazette') will give you a sufficient overview so as to be able to contribute to conversations and ask intelligent questions and that all adds loads to your credibility.

Of course, talking is all well and good but it's the listening that really holds the key in developing relationships.

Listening

Earlier on, we made reference to the fact that we live in an age where we are bombarded by people and organisations attempting to get our attention.

In this state, we hear everything but listen to nothing. It's akin to sitting in front of a conveyor belt of information: we see it but register very little.

However, when you want to get to know someone, when you are looking out for the next client, when you are at the 'Acknowledgement' bit at the base of the triangle and want to see if it might go all the way to 'Respect', In other words, CONNECT with them, you HAVE to listen to them: listen to seek to understand.

- Bond
- Trust
- Respect
- Acceptance
- Understanding
- Acknowledgement

In short then: you hear with your ears but you listen with your eyes.

Really listening means listening and deriving meaning from what's said. Often, particularly in networking situations, we get so fixated on what we think we should be telling the prospect about our service, we are not listening to what the other person's saying but focusing on how to 'sell' how we might help!

Minimal encouragers are the barely perceptible expressions we make when listening – the slight raise of an eyebrow, nod of our head or noise of agreement 'Ugh-hum', etc.

Equally, we tend to move closer to people, ideas and objects to which we are attracted and farther away from those we aren't. This move 'toward' or 'away' may be minute and yet we are sensitive to it. There is even when the two parties are close enough, a very slight change in air pressure!

The thing to always remember, when conversing with another person, is that it's not about you! It's about them and how they feel.

The most important feeling with which you can leave them is they feel as though they have been heard!

Kissing: To Kiss or Not to Kiss?

People in Europe love a bit of cheek action – blokes and women alike but we Brits are not too sure about it; particularly, in a business setting.

Here's what we've observed travelling up and down the country.

Men in business do not kiss each other.

Women in business do not kiss each other – unless they know each other really well.

Women in London kiss each other – one kiss on each cheek but only when they know one another well.

Women in London will kiss a bloke they know well – one on each cheek.

When Nick is in London and meets a woman he knows very well in London he will kiss her on both cheeks. If the relationship is with a woman who is outside of the capital, it tends to be only the one cheek. (The two cheek thing seems to be limited to within the M25.)

Men and women we don't know well or have never met before, we shake hands.

From a guy's perspective, in the case of female clients, there does come a point when the relationship has moved from handshake to kiss, in which case Nick tends to shake their hand and kiss them. The 'kiss barrier' is then broken and from then on that's the greeting both parties tend to follow.

If in doubt: don't kiss – no matter how well you know one another in a business context. If you feel awkward about it then you'll pass those uncertain feelings on to her and then it's not pleasant for either party and you both end up worrying about when you part following the meeting or when you next meet again, whether you should kiss or not.

If in doubt then leave it out BUT you must greet and acknowledge everyone you meet, irrespective of gender!

We now want to tackle how to follow up after meeting someone at an event, be that formal or informal.

We know this is a bit of an awkward one for a great number of people, which is why we are going to share a step-by-step procedure you can follow, which is guaranteed to make you far more confident.

CONNECT – Examples of Letters and Emails

Examples of Letters

Letter One

Hello Mary

A couple of months ago I contacted your firm to find out who was responsible for training and was told that up until recently the firm didn't really have a training policy as such and that it was all a bit "ad hoc". However, the lady I spoke to quickly went on to say that they would all change because "a new lady, called Mary is starting with us on the 12th of October".

Not wanting to bother you by calling at what must be a very hectic time, I have opted to send you some information about what I do.

I'm a former lawyer and director of a legal recruitment company, which means I understand how frustrating it can sometimes be trying to persuade a bunch of highly intelligent solicitors just how vital it is that they are relaxed and chatty at a networking event and equally, that a 45-slide PowerPoint presentation just isn't going to woo a potential client in a pitch for business. What I deliver is practical, down-to-earth training that people enjoy and learn from; all delivered without the use of PowerPoint!

Mary, I'm sure you will have training providers in mind already, to deliver various elements of oral communication skills and that it will be some time before you are in a position to put together a coherent training package for every member of staff, however, I am writing to you now because I am in the north-west on a few occasions over the next couple of months, meeting up with the HR and training managers of a number of the significant law firms. As such I am very keen to pop in and see you since Preston Partners is one of the major partnerships in the area.

To that end, I will give you a ring in the next week or so to see whether you are in a position to put something in your diary.

Thanks a lot

Letter Two

Hello Rebecca

We spoke on Thursday and chatted briefly about me sending you some info about what I do and the joys that await me in raising two boys for the next 11 years.

So, whilst my two run around a campsite in the Loire Valley and I attempt to read at least one book in two weeks, you can cast your eyes over my blurb.

I deliver training to a wide variety of organisations but my background in law and legal recruitment means that I spend an awful lot of my time helping lawyers polish up their communication skills – whether that be in delivering seminars, pitching for business or networking.

I work with some thumpingly large global law firms as well as some smaller ones just in Aberdeen but all appreciate that possessing technical legal skills simply isn't enough if they are going to stand out from the crowd and compete in today's market.

I'm coming to the north of England over the next few months to talk to a number of partnerships and would like to include you in my rounds if you have 40 minutes to spare. That way you can tell me what kind of training provision you make for your people in the firm and find out whether what I do might help, now or in the future.

Thanks a lot

Letter Three

Hello Vicky

I met up with Dave a couple of weeks ago and he treated me to a spot of lunch and we chatted about Spurs and Morgans. However, he also remarked that if he'd given it a bit of thought, it would have been a good idea for you and me to have a chat whilst I was there.

Anyway, until that happens, I thought it'd be useful to send you my card plus a biog, along with the outlines of the sort of training I do for law firms.

It would be great to meet up, so I'll give you a ring in the next week or so and perhaps we can put something in the diary.

Regards

Letter Four

Good morning, Bill

Mary Goodnight and I met up on Tuesday the 27th of January and had a chat about training and related matters and whilst there is nothing I can help her with at the moment, she did say that it might well be worth you and me catching up.

I'll not bore you with the details Bill but suffice to say that 99.9% of the work I do is with lawyers and would-be lawyers. I train and coach from pre-LPC students, right through to very senior equity partners who bill out at £800 per hour.

What I do is help make them better business developers and ambassadors for their firms, be that through delivering better pitches or following up after networking events. Indeed, it is my course, 'Beyond the Business Card' that Linda specifically thought you might be interested in learning more about, which addresses that bit that all lawyers seem to find tricky – turning networking contacts into business.

I work with a whole bunch of firms ranging in size from 'Massive' to 'Large and Massive' to little eight partner firms in Edinburgh and with lawyers from across the globe.

For clients with whom I do regular work, I reduce my fees by 15% as well.

It'd be great to find another excuse to come to Liverpool – although I'm a Manc, I do love the place – so I'll be in touch in the next few days to see if we can put a date in the diary to have a chat over a coffee.

Cheers

Examples of Emails

Email One

Hello Venessa

We are scheduled to have a chat over a coffee on the 6th of April at 2 pm. However, in my stupidity and general blokeiness, I have realised that this is slap-bang in the middle of my Easter break with my wife and two boys!

Whilst, I really like coming to Bristol and do so want to meet up, I'm afraid time with my family just wins the 'what would you rather be doing' race. So, if it's not too much of a pain, could we re-arrange? How are you fixed for the 28th of April?

Yours, rather foolishly
Nick

Email Two

> Hi Simon
>
> I trust all is well with you and that the Newly qualified/trainee 'season' is going smoothly.
>
> It's been a good few months since I was recumbent in one of your exotic pieces of furniture and thought I should drop you a line to see where you were up to regarding the possibility of coming in and working with your lawyers.
>
> I'm especially mindful that as the party season approaches, lawyers always tend to need to be a tad sharper at the old networking and following up and to make the most of their schmoosing.
>
> Will leave it with you Simon and if you feel another natter is appropriate, let me know; as you know I am always around and about the City. I'll drop you a line in six weeks if I've heard nowt from you.
>
> Cheers

Email Three

> Hi Martin
>
> Just the briefest of emails to say how good it was to get a chance to have a natter with you yesterday.
>
> It'd be great to meet up again, either with you or a colleague to learn more about how you guys go about training and whether what I do might be of help. However, I'll wait to hear from you and only get in touch in about six weeks if I've not.
>
> Cheers

Email Four

> Hi Kate
>
> Just a quick note to say how lovely it was to see you and not have to even buy you a cup of coffee! You are always so upbeat and smiley, which is like of breath of fresh air with so many dull people about nowadays.
>
> Speak soon and have fun.

Regarding your hairdresser: maybe just take her to local places first, such as the end of the District or Central line. Then, when you get there you can sit on a park bench and she can do your hair in readiness for the return journey. You could even really spoil her and buy her; her very own Oyster card!

Her reply,

Excellent email, Nick – you had me laughing out loud. I'll definitely pass the suggestion on to my hairdresser!

It was good to see you and catch up about so many different topics in a short space of time.

See you soon no doubt.

Kate

Email Five

Subject: Tony Wilson – 'We do things differently here'

Hello Paul

We've never met – although I have seen your pic on LinkedIn.

I am getting in touch because I would like to have a chat with you over Zoom, find out how you go about improving the skills of your fee earners and see whether what I do might help.

Ordinarily, I have given you a ring in the office and sent you some stuff in the post but with things being a bit up in the air, I reckoned an email might well do the trick.

Anyway, aside from letting you know I used to be a lawyer in Hammond Suddards' Manchester office on John Dalton Street – I am a 'Manc' now living in Edinburgh – I have attached a short biog so you get an idea of what I do and with whom I do it.

I shall leave it with you and drop you a line in a couple of weeks if I've not heard a peep.

Cheers
Nick

PS – Oh and here's a link to videos I have on YouTube – me 'in action' so to speak.

Hi Nick,

A conversation would be more relevant in December time if you want to get back in touch then. However, in the meantime, in addition to your biog, it would also be helpful if you could let us know how you are delivering learning virtually.

Many thanks and do feel free to get back in touch in December.

Kind regards
Paul

YOU can even inject your personality into a formal proposal and when mentioning money. This is the final paragraph of a detailed proposal Nick put together for the contract to train all the fee-earners at a law firm, in a range of communication and sales skills.

The money

'I like to be dead upfront about money and avoid all the flowery stuff favoured by many when quoting.

My full-day rate is £X and my half-day is £X, both plus VAT.

That includes expenses – rail, plane, taxi, dromedary, hotel, food, Innocent smoothies: the whole nine yards. It also includes preparation, bespoke, tailoring, whittling down, enlarging and any phone calls/meetings that I have to have with you in order to make this stuff bang on for you and those funky little booklets. (The one on presentation skills is being put together as we speak.)

BUT and it's a lovely, cuddly, warm, fluffy "BUT", because you would be committing to so much work and because you have come and found me and have done such a huge amount of groundwork I am more than delighted: nay, chuffed, to reduce my rates to:

£X for a full day and £X for a half.

Now having had a look at your schedule I reckon that you need X days of training, comprising a mix of full and half days, which comes to a fun-sized £X plus VAT, which represents a £X saving from my standard daily rate for you and means that I can tell my two, puppy-eyed children that they will get presents this Christmas'.

Following Up after a Networking Event

Let's be clear on this point again.

Following up is something you should do AT EVERY STAGE OF THE BUSINESS DEVELOPMENT PROCESS. It's part of the 'ask' process.

At each and every stage you must let people know what you are going to do next and when you are going to do it! EVERY SINGLE TIME!

You are NOT going to wish to follow up and secure and meeting with everyone you chat to.

You are probably only going to want to arrange that all-important, third stage of the model 'meet', with those who meet two criteria:

1. You like them and have enjoyed their company.
2. Think the services you offer could be of help to them or those they know.

You are NOT attempting to secure a date in their diary in order to 'sell' to them but to learn more about them, their role, organisation and then, only if you think there is something you offer and would be of benefit to them, will you tell them about it.

Many people attend events, get chatting to a few people, come away with cards and LinkedIn connections wishing to follow up with the suggestion of a coffee or lunch but because they feel awkward, never do.

That's because they are unsure as to how to approach them – phone, email or direct message, and how long to wait before doing so. Which is why they end up putting them on a mailing list, ensuring they receive updates, sector briefings, newsletters, invites to seminars and the ubiquitous e-card at Christmas.

How to do it?

We've honed and perfected this over the past decades and it works. Sure, amend it, make it personal to you but don't deviate too far from it. We've built a successful business from a standing start doing it.

It works if you want to break into a new market, a new sector or a new geographical area. It works if you are starting from scratch or developing a bigger market share in one familiar to you already.

The most important point here is to lay the foundations for setting up the follow up chat, whilst you're still talking to the person.

When you are chatting to someone at an event, the relationship is 'hot'. Once you shake hands and part company, it begins to cool.

Most people will email a day or two later with something similar to the following:

'Hi Anwar, it was great meeting you at the event a couple of days ago: I hope you managed to catch the last train?

Next time you are in town, it might be nice to catch up for a cup of coffee so do let me know when's convenient'.

This is not ideal in a couple of respects.

First, you are attempting to 'warm' Anwar up to a point where he is respective to a cup of coffee, which is harder to do via email than it is in person and, second, whilst being undeniably polite, it is quite the opposite of 'keeping control'.

This is how to do it far more effectively:

Step One

Whilst you are still at the networking event/meeting/social, whatever.

You: Anwar, it's been great meeting you and have a chat. I've been really interested in what you had to say about (your firm/your business/ your plans for the future), and it'd be great to continue our conversation over a coffee, and find out more about what you do.

Or

You: It's been great to meet you Anwar and hear about what you do. Listen, next time I'm in this neck of the woods we should get together over a coffee and have a natter; it'd be interesting to learn more.

These are not definitive. There's no set script! We do not want you to learn this and quote it verbatim; you will find your own form of words but make sure you keep it relaxed and light.

You will notice there is no talk about having a 'meeting' or arranging an 'appointment', preferring reference to 'coffee'. 'Coffee' conjures up informal, neutral, no pressure, which is exactly what it should be.

However, the really important bit here, the bit you cannot miss out, is the fact you are lining up a follow up meeting right there and then, rather than waiting a few days and then trying to do it.

Having suggested you could meet up sometime over a coffee, Anwar's reply will almost certainly be...

"Yeah, sure, that'd be nice".

It would be most uncomfortable for someone to look you eye at this point and say "NO": it's just too rude.

If they don't want to meet up they will let you know but not right there and then: they'll do that later and by email – which is fine (but more of that later on).

So let's assume Anwar agrees.

You: Great, I'll give you a ring before the end of the week/beginning of the next and we'll put a date in the diary.

If the time frame you've stated is not good for them, "Oh, not next week because I'm on holiday", tell them you'll get in touch the following week.

There's also another closing technique hidden in there. Did you spot it?

Read it again.

It's something called 'The assumptive close'.

You have neither asked, 'When shall I ring you to set something up? or said '...to see if you would be free to meet up for a coffee'.

What you've said – quite deliberately – is "I'll give you a ring before the end of the week/beginning of next" followed by "and we'll put a date in the diary". You have assumed this meeting is going to go ahead!

You then part company and either later on at the event or on your way home or in the office the next day, note down the salient points of information you picked up during the small talk, in particular, anything they are doing or are involved with prior to when you've said you will get in touch. You do this so that when you do, you have something to say by way of an introduction:

"How did your trip to Swansea go?"

"I remember you mentioned you were going to a wedding last weekend, how did it go?"

People like to know they have been listened to, so not only is this kind of question a relaxed and non-pressured way to get the conversation going, it lets the other person know you were listening to them and that fact alone will put you in the top 10% of people they've ever met at a networking event! It builds rapport and that's what good salespeople do.

Step Two: The 'Holding' Email

Once you've done the 'It would be great to meet up sometime over a coffee', to which they have agreed, and then you've said, 'I'll ring before the end of the week, on my return to the office', it is sometimes useful to send the 'holding email', which goes along these lines:

"Hi Anwar, Nick here – the tall Mancunian bloke with a thing for shoes – just a quick note to say how nice it was to meet you yesterday/earlier on and to let you know that I'll be in touch before the end of the week to fix a date up for that coffee".

Again, you'll note the tone is relaxed and informal and you are giving her a quick prompt as to who you are. It would be odd to have chatted with Anwar, exchanged small talk and presumably got on but then sent him a more formal email, such as something like the one below:

> Good afternoon, Anwar
>
> It was really nice to meet you yesterday evening at the 'Lawyers in the City' meeting at The Chandlers Hall.
>
> I am very keen to meet up and talk to you about the full range of strategic business improvement models and techniques and how I think they might be of help to your business.
>
> I will give you a call later on in the week in order to arrange an appointment to have a meeting at a time that is convenient for you.
>
> Kind regards
> Nick Davies

It's too formal. And to be frank, the idea of having a coffee with someone who is going to tell him about the 'strategic business improvement models' they offer is too dreary for words.

Step two is also important because it highlights two things you must always do when promoting your services; both of which we've mentioned several times so far:

- Tell them what you are going to do next.
- Tell them when you are going to do it.

People in business loathe surprises. Let your prospect know at every single step of the process what it is you are going to do and when you're going to do it.

Step Three

Do what you said you'd do and when you said you'd do it.

If you said you'd drop them an email before the end of the week then guess what.....? Ditto if you said you'd give them a ring. If you just said you'd 'be in touch', then either option's open to you, however, the phone is more immediate and is different from what all your competitors are doing.

To some of you reading this, you may be thinking the phone is somehow 'old-fashioned' or perhaps too pushy.

However, we'd urge you not to dismiss it!

The phone has a number of advantages:

- It's quicker than typing
- There is an opportunity for small talk not so naturally available via email or direct message

- Someone's voice is rich in tone, pace, volume, rhythm, pitch and timbre, which means you can more readily sense their feelings towards meeting up (email contains none of this vital insight)

Anyone can say that they 'love you' but you know if they mean it by the way they say it and how they behave.

What's more – and here's where you want to be a little assertive – it's harder for someone to say "No" to you over the phone if they've changed their mind. This is a little, tiny bit of pressure but that's ok.

The phone call

You phone, you get through – here's what you say:

You: Hi Anwar, it's Nick here, you recall we met the other evening at the "X event"; I'm the guy that used to be a lawyer and has a thing about shoes. We chatted about…

You need merely refresh their memory since they might well have met any number of people since meeting you. There's nothing worse than someone calling you and they start going on about something, whilst all the while you're trying to work out who they are, let alone when you met them!

Once they've placed you, now's a good time to either indulge in a little small talk and refer back to things that you made a note of or get straight to the point.

Again, there are no hard and fast rules to this: you'll sense that some people are up for a bit of chat and others aren't; it depends on what mood they're in. At first, you aren't going to get this right every time, but don't beat yourself up about it: the more you do it the better you'll get.

Once any small talk is done or if small talk seems inappropriate, you need to tell them why you are calling.

You: Anyway I'm calling to arrange a time for that coffee we talked about and wondered whether later this week or next week was best?

You are being upfront and straight to the point. You are not using aggressive language or tone but you do know what you want. They did say they were up for it and they did know you were going to get in touch to arrange something (no surprises, remember). You are also using the alternative close.

You get voicemail.

You have to leave a message.

We have already talked about 'Trust' and 'Credibility' being the essential ingredients necessary for effective persuasion.

If you have told them you will call before the end of the week, you must do just that, because if you don't, it sows a tiny seed of doubt in their mind as to whether you are a person of your word.

The message needs to include the following:

- Your name
- Where you met
- Why you are calling – to set up a time to meet
- What you are going to do next
- Your number

You: Hi Anwar, it's Nick here. You recall we met last Thursday at the Lawyers in the City doo; I was the tall Mancunian bloke that commented on your great shoes. Anyway, I'm ringing to put a date in the diary to meet up and have a natter, as I said I would. I'll try you again later this week but in the meantime, if you get a minute then you can always give me a call. My number is 0777 777 777. Thanks.

This is a bit like the 'holding email' in that it's relaxed and informal but also assumes that you will meet up. However, it adds your number because if he rings back: BINGO!

If you leave a message and a potential client calls you that's what salespeople refer to as a 'BUYING SIGN'.

It's very rare someone will call you back to say they have changed their mind – they'll normally prefer email for that, so if you do get a call it usually means they are interested. 'Interested' in meeting up, that is. Yes, they might have an inclination you might well be able to provide them something they need but the only thing you want them to be interested in at this point is meeting up with you.

This is an important point: a very important point. DO NOT GO SELLING YOUR WARES OVER THE TELEPHONE OR VIA EMAIL.

The ONLY THING you are 'selling' here is a chat over a coffee. All you want, the only thing you want from them is their time.

They know you are not meeting up for a social. They also know that ultimately you would like them to use your services: they're not stupid but thus far you've made it all so relaxed and pleasant that they are happy to meet up.

We said it earlier on in the book but people buy from people they like and that selling is about making it easy for people to buy. If arranging to meet up with you is easy and pleasant then the chances are working with you will be just the same.

What you are doing right from the first meeting – formal or informal – is letting the person know that you would be easy to work with.

Step Four (If They've Not Replied)

Leave it a week or perhaps a little bit longer before you try again. Somewhere between a week and two weeks is best.

If they pick up the phone; you're off. If not, leave a voice mail similar to the first one but add that you are 'still keen to meet up'.

Step Five (If You Still Haven't Heard Back)

Another couple of weeks go by and still, nothing?

Email

This is what the follow-up stages look like thus far:

1 Telephone
2 Telephone
3 Email

The email should be similar to the voicemail you've left. Informal, relaxed, chatty and contain the same info – tell them why you are emailing and tell them what you are going to do next.

The only thing to add in the email is a bit about the fact that you've already tried to get hold of them via phone.

A typical email would go like this:

> Hi Anwar
>
> I've left a couple of voicemails over the past few weeks but with no luck, so thought I'd send you an email since I know that sometimes it's a lot less hassle to reply than setting aside time to make a call.
>
> I'm still dead keen to meet up and have a chat and am in your area on the 6th and 7th of July so hopefully, we can put a date in the diary.
>
> In the meantime, I've put some stuff about what I do in the post to give you a better feel for what it is I do.
>
> Nick

Once again, it's relaxed and you are using a laid-back alternative close by suggesting some dates. If he comes back and says he cannot do those dates you know he's looked in his diary, which tells you he's interested.

You are also telling him what you are going to do next – send him some stuff about the services you provide.

Notice also that you have not used the word 'brochure' or 'literature'. Literature is what Jane Austin, Dickens and Thackery produced: you don't. Sometimes you might prefer the term 'info.' or 'information'.

In a minute, we take a look in detail at the types of covering letters Nick has sent with 'info' but at this stage, it's important to appreciate the importance of email.

The really great thing about email at this point in the process is that it allows the person you wish to meet, to say "No". And you want it to be easy for them to say "NO".

Right at the beginning of this section, it's highly unlikely someone would say 'no' when you suggested, at the end of your initial chat with them at the networking event, that you met up for a coffee the next time you were in their area. You may also recall that if they weren't interested, they'd tell you later. Well, this is when they'll do it.

If someone you are talking to agrees – albeit informally – to meet up for a chat at some point in the future, it is terribly difficult for them to then turn you down when you ring and speak to them. Human beings like to be consistent and agreeing to something and then subsequently changing their mind is a really awkward thing to do.

However, if we do change our mind it's so much easier to do via email because it distances us from the message.

Of course, the response to your email will not be, 'Sorry Nick but I've changed my mind and I don't want to meet for a chat over a coffee', it'll be delivered with a little excuse:

> Hi Nick
>
> Sorry, I've not been back to you earlier (they will always apologise for not having returned your call) but things are a bit hectic here, what with graduate recruitment and apprentice induction.
>
> I wonder if we might put meeting up on hold for the time being until I can get some breathing space in my diary?

This is Ok. Don't take it personally, don't get upset and don't get defensive or pushy. They are obviously too busy and quite frankly you don't want to be wasting time – theirs or yours – sitting and drinking coffee if they don't want to be there.

But don't give up.

You must acknowledge their message with something like this:

> No worries at all Anwar: I completely understand.
>
> When's best for me to get back in touch; October or perhaps the start of next year (make these 'dates' roughly three and six months apart.)
>
> In the meantime you've got all my info, so if anything comes up that I can help you with then give me a shout.
>
> Nick

Relaxed and informal. It's no big deal he doesn't want to see you YET. He is not saying, 'NEVER', just not yet. Note you are using the alternative close again and telling him what you are going to do and offering him an alternative as to when you're going to do it.

On the majority of occasions, the person will come back to you and have selected one or two of the options, in which case a note should be made in your diary, together with confirmation you will be in touch when he suggests.

You should always be trying to 'leave the door open' to get back in touch. Never shut things off completely because you never know what's going to happen and neither do they: circumstances change.

The Letter

The letter is one of the steps in the follow-up process you may wish to consider. There is no hard and fast rule as to when to send it. You might send it following the first or second voicemail and occasionally after the first email.

The following is an example letter:

> Hello James
>
> I've called a couple of times to try and speak to you but with no luck, so yesterday – the 29th – I left a voicemail to let you know I'd be sending you some information about what I do – here it is.
>
> I'm a former lawyer and have worked with many thousands of lawyers, which means I understand how frustrating it can sometimes be trying to persuade a bunch of highly intelligent solicitors just how vital it is that they are relaxed and chatty and networking events and equally, that a 45-slide PowerPoint presentation just isn't going to woo a potential client in a pitch for business. What I deliver is practical, down-to-earth training that people enjoy and learn from; all delivered without the use of PowerPoint.
>
> Although I've delivered training to all the major law firms in The City, I've yet to do things for firms in the North West, which is a crying shame since I'm a Mancunian now living in Edinburgh but always keen to 'go home'. I also know there are some cracking partnerships there as well.
>
> I have appointments to meet the HR/Training managers of about eight firms in the region over the next couple of months and would really like to pop in and chat with you, find out how you go about training and whether what I do might help.
>
> I'll give you a call in the next few days and, hopefully, we can put something in the diary.
>
> Regards

The usual elements are there:

- Humour
- Establishing credibility
- Telling him why I'm contacting him and what I want
- Letting him know what I'm going to do next and when

Step Six: If You Still Haven't Heard a Thing – The 'Pain in the Back-Side' Email

You've left two messages on their voicemail. You've sent an email and written a letter with some of your company info along with it but alas, no response. What should you do? Give up? Call it a day?

You've got to face facts, they are either very busy or really don't want to see you, either way, you must find out.

In this kind of case, an email like this is superb!

(I have deleted the guy's surname so as not to embarrass him):

> To: Kevin
>
> Subject: A bit of a pain
>
> Morning, Kevin
>
> I'm still keen to meet up and have a chat. However, following a couple of voicemails, a letter and an email, I'm acutely aware of rapidly becoming a pain in the backside.
>
> So, I'll not be bothering you again until the start of next year, when I'll get in touch just to see where you're up to and whether my timing is better.
>
> Regards
> Nick
>
> (He replied less than an hour later).
>
> To: Nick
>
> Subject: RE: A bit of a pain
>
> Hi Nick,
>
> Not at all Nick.

> Apologies for not coming back to you, things are rather hectic at the moment. I received your literature and as yet have not read it. Perhaps you could give me a call in a month and we can take it from there.
>
> Regards
> Kevin

Roughly half of the people you send this to will reply and the majority of them apologise profusely for having not got back to you sooner. Some will then go on to suggest a date, whilst others acknowledge they are very busy and they appreciate the fact you've recognised that fact.

The other 50%, to which you do not receive a reply, you simply say…

"NEXT!"

Never beg for business. Even if winning this client would be the deal of the century. Even if you've lain awake at night imagining being able to tell people that you got the X account: don't ever seem desperate for their business.

Keen; yes! Focused; yes! Determined; most definitely but never desperate. Needy people are very unattractive.

MEET

Why MEET?

When setting up meetings, try and stick to language that's more relaxed: 'coffee', 'natter', 'chat', 'get-together', etc. However, it seemed daft to have all of those as a title, which is why we have nevertheless titled this, 'The Meeting'.

The purpose of this meeting is to find out about the person, their role, more about the business, and whether what you have on offer might be of interest to them.

Some people get bogged down in listing lots and lots of questions in such meetings. We don't, for us, this is more about seeing whether we get on but with a bit of information gathering on the side, rather than being our principal focus.

VENUE

Unless circumstances dictate otherwise, you should always plump for going to visit them. It shows you are keen and prepared to go out of your way, you learn loads more and because they are 'At home', they're relaxed, which means more open and more forthcoming.

In a world in which communicating virtually is easy, convenient and incurs very little cost, it's understandable many favour it.

However, going the 'extra mile', sometimes, literally means that! Remember, your competitor may well have been bothered to go and see the client you are chasing. You don't want to be seen as less keen!

Going to their place also opens up the possibility of meeting other relevant people within their organisation whilst you're there.

A while back Nick visited a firm in Bristol to meet the HR and training manager with whom he was getting on really well, when they mentioned that although they wished to go ahead and use him to do some training, it was their boss, 'David', who had the final say so. So naturally, Nick asked if it would be possible just to say 'hello', to him, if he was in the office.

As it happens he wasn't available. However, it's always worth asking.

If going to their place is not an option, a coffee shop convenient for them should be your next venue of choice. Always pay, or at least, offer to pay. It's polite and brings in a nice bit of reciprocity.

TAKING OTHER PEOPLE ALONG

There might be occasions when you think the person you are meeting would benefit from seeing one of your colleagues at the same time.

Whilst you shouldn't rule this out, you must always ask them if they mind. To turn up without having run it passed them could be viewed as a tad pushy. You must explain to the person you are meeting, why you think it would be of benefit to them to meet this second guest.

A partner at a law firm with whom Nick recently worked told a story of having come from an in-house role, inviting a former colleague to meet for lunch, just to make sure the relationship was still strong and to see if there was a possibility of him being given work from his previous firm, only to have two partners get wind of it and invite themselves along for the meal.

Whilst sure their intentions were well-meaning, their new colleague felt awkward at turning up 'mob-handed' but not half as uncomfortable as his former colleague who felt as though he had been ambushed and was being press-ganged into pushing business their way. Three to one is not fair!

COFFEE OR LUNCH?

Coffee.

Lunch could be construed as too formal, it can be difficult to make notes during lunch and it commits them to at least an hour and a half and is perhaps too intimate at the beginning of a relationship. Plus, it could end up costing a bit, depending on what the order is!

Before You Set Off

This is obvious stuff but make sure you know where you're going. If they have more than one office, check to see which one they are expecting to meet you at.

Boot up the sat-nav, navigation app, and be sure of your route and how you are going to get there – bus, cab, tube, plane, etc. And make sure you know how long it will take and then add some time to allow for delays, hold-ups and missed trains.

If your journey is disrupted, be sure to let your prospective client know!

Professional salespeople are rarely late because they understand the important role trust and dependability play in securing business.

In fact, let me tell you a story that illustrates my point and tells you something about how salespeople regard training as well.

Example

A few years back Nick delivered a one-day's course on presentation skills to three senior sales managers. It was held in a small conference room at a hotel adjacent to Heathrow Airport.

The course began at 9.30 am. One of the delegates had flown from Huston, Texas, the other from Rio de Janeiro and another from Dubai. With the exception of the guy from Texas, who had mistakenly booked a ticket to Gatwick, telephoned Nick, apologised and explained he'd be 15 minutes late (in the event he was 12), they turned up on time, participated in the course and then flew back to their respective home cities.

Salespeople hate being late and even if they have to fly halfway across the world to learn something new, they will, if they think that'll give them the edge over their competitors.

People, who take developing business seriously, are always looking for the edge. Stephen Covey in his renowned book, 'The 7 Habits of Highly Effective People', lists habit number 7 as 'Sharpen the Saw'. In other words, keep learning and give yourself the edge.

Get into the habit of ensuring you have a pen, paper, diary, business card and any other information about your firm you need to take.

You may have seen an article in a newspaper written by an employee or perhaps one featuring the company as a whole. In either case, make a note of the salient points. These sorts of things can be great to help move the conversation from small to business talk.

In the same vein, take a look at their profile on LinkedIn and the company website.

The latter will give you a feel for the organisation, what it does, in which sectors, where their offices are and whilst you're at it, put all that information into your CRM (Client Relationship Management) system, if you have one.

You don't need to know everything!

Chances are the potential client will ask, how much you know of their organisation, to which you must be able to demonstrate a little.

Nick often says something along these lines…

> I've looked at your website and have a good understanding of what you do and the markets in which you operate but one of the reasons I wanted to pop in and see you was to get a much better feel of what your organisation is about and the way you go about doing things.

Email to Confirm

A day, or even a couple of days prior to the meeting, send an email to them just to check that all's well to go ahead as arranged.

Example

Nick learned this valuable lesson way back in his early days being a seas rep in the late eighties!

He set off at 5 o'clock in the morning to drive from Manchester for a 9.30 meeting in Norwich, at which it had already been agreed that a contract was going to be signed that meant a decent amount of commission for Nick!

He arrived only to have the bloke sit him in his office and tell him he'd changed his mind!

On the Day

As you've probably sussed by now – and it's an obvious one – get to their offices early. Ten minutes is good. If it's raining go into reception and let them know you are early and not to contact the person you're meeting because they may feel under pressure to hurry to finish whatever they are doing.

You know what it's like. If you've arranged for someone to come to your house at 10 and they turn up at 9.30, it can really throw you off if you're not prepared.

If, on the other hand, you are able to see someone perhaps up to an hour prior to the agreed time, it's worth dropping them an email to ask if bringing it forwarded would suit them better. Occasionally it does and quite often they're really pleased.

Make sure when you do get in touch you make it clear you are very happy to stick with the agreed time and that you are simply giving them the option of the earlier time because it might be helpful and more convenient for them.

In Reception

Ok, you have gone to reception and let the person behind the desk know you've arrived.

Although increasingly rare, the first thing they will ask you to do is sign the visitor's book.

This little, much over-looked book is a font of useful information, so when you sign in, make sure you take your time to complete each section nicely, neatly and slowly because as you write in your details you should be scanning the page to see who else has visited the company and more importantly, the person you're going to be meeting. In particular, you are looking to see if any of your competitors have been calling.

What you learn here is not going to form the basis of any conversation you have with your potential client but is nice background stuff to have in mind.

Once the book is signed and you have in your possession the security pass, you should ask the receptionist where the loo is; even if you don't need to go. Wash your hands, check your hair, your teeth, your nose, that buttons, zips and ties are done up and that your shoes are clean.

Once back in reception, try and avoid sitting down.

Modern reception furniture is lovely isn't it: huge, comfy sofas in black leather: The sort you can sink right into, settle back, grab a paper from the glass coffee table and get comfy with. Mmm, nice!

All true, except there's a downside: they are devilishly hard from which to extricate yourself! Plus, when you meet your contact, you'll be seated law down, whilst they are standing and, you really want to be meeting them on the same level, so the relationship gets off on equal terms.

STAND in reception.

Do glance through any material, brochures or info regarding the organisation, which may be placed on the coffee table.

DO LOOK at any awards they may have displayed. These will provide nice opening topics of conversation.

If you are asked to wait in the meeting room for the person you are seeing DO NOT SIT DOWN. Wait until they come in and indicate where they are going to sit before you plump for your seat.

Accept a drink. Even if it's water and you just sip it: it's polite and creates a more relaxed environment.

THE VIEW – I visit loads of offices that occupy floors many stories high and more often than not, that makes for a decent view.

Comment on it to your host when they enter the room. It's a nice little, relaxed opener and you'll be amazed how many people join you at the window and start giving a bird's-eye view tour of the vista before you.

In the Meeting

You've both settled in. Drinks have been poured, biscuits selected and it's time to kick things off with a bit of small talk.

They will normally kick things off with 'Did you find us alright?' or 'So, how did you get here – train/walk/bike/car, etc.'.

If you've done the 'what a delightful view' bit, then the other small-talk standards are fine.

If there are photos of their kids on the wall or paintings done by their kids, comment on them.

Eventually, however, the small talk has to cease and the business at hand must be addressed.

A nice little segue into more business-related topics might be: 'So, how long have you been at the company?'. Or 'Reading your LinkedIn profile, I notice you used to be with/you studied at/you were formerly...'

Of course, at some point, you are going to wish to take control of proceedings, in which case...

"Well, I know you're very busy so first of all thanks for giving up the time" and then reiterate why I wanted to see them in the first place:

> I really wanted to learn more about the way you go about improving the performance of your company and the plans for the next few years, as well as find out more about the organisation other than that I've picked up from your website.

Often the person will ask you what you know of their business and it's at this point you'd mention some of the stuff you'd managed to glean from when you did your research.

Asking Questions

We strongly suggest you consider the kinds of questions you want to know the answers to, prior to going into the meeting and even write them down so you don't forget. Once you get confident with these sorts of meetings, you'll find yourself asking roughly similar questions each time. However, as with the stuff on small talk, it's the listening that's more important than the questions.

Of course, what you wish to ask will be determined by what you hope to get from the meeting and, then, as the meeting progresses, by the answers you receive to those questions.

It would be daft to try and list all the possible questions you could ask in such a meeting but here are a few general ones, applicable, no matter what it is you're selling:

- What/who do you use at the moment?
- How did that relationship come about?
- What do you like about your current supplier?
- Is there anything you'd change about the service/product you currently receive/use (this questions on from number '3' but it would not be right to ask 'What don't you like about them?' So, this is a more delicate way of finding out.
- What's the annual spend on these products/this service?
- Who else is in your department?
- When will the supplier list be reviewed?
- Other than you, who else is involved in the decision as to which supplier to use?*
- What kind of relationship do you want with your suppliers?**

WHY?

Why is 'Why' not included in the list of questions?'

A 'why' question is best avoided if possible because when you ask somebody 'why' they chose to follow a particular course of action or made a decision, you are asking them to justify that decision. And when you do that you immediately put them on the defensive and that's something you wish to avoid when attempting to influence and persuade them to use your services.

Once again, this is all about how you phrase things.

Words are seriously important, in that the meaning you intended to convey may not be the meaning interpreted by the receiver. You must choose your words carefully and phrase things in such a way as to reflect the way your listener speaks. You can only achieve that by listening to them.

We are all familiar with phrases such as 'that rings a bell' or 'I see what you mean' and 'We need to get a grip of the situation'.

These are examples of what is perhaps best termed 'sensory language' and you can copy it to help establish rapport, quickly and easily. In fact, this auditory 'mirroring' is the technique hostages use to help build rapport with hostage takers.

Roughly speaking, 40% of the population favours 'auditory' words and phrases, another 40% have a preference for 'visual' with the remaining 20% preferring what's known as 'kinaesthetic' language.

Question Examples

Auditory

'I like the sound of that'
'Singing from the same song sheet'
'He dropped a clanger'
'That really chimes with me'
'It's important we get the tone right'

Visual

'We share a clear vision'
'I need more clarity'
'There's light at the end of the tunnel'
'She's looking at it through rose-tinted glasses'
'Looks good to me!'

Kinaesthetic

'We need to get a grip on this'
'Don't let this opportunity slip through your fingers'
'My gut feeling is…'
'He really needs to get his feet back on the ground!'
'We find ourselves in a tight spot'

* 'Other than you, who else is involved in the decision as to which supplier to use'

You need to find out who makes the decision AND who signs off the money. They may be two different people and you need to know.

If you are sitting in front of the decision maker but not the person with the cash, you need to ask them, one, the name of that individual, and two, whether they can arrange to meet up with them; the name of the MAN in other words.

Let's say Anwar tells you he's the decision-maker but has to run costs by Holly, you need to ask – there and then – whether Holly is about and whether you can meet her.

There's another reason for this too. You are always going to be the best person to sell what you are offering. Anwar may love what you do but with all the will in the world, he cannot convey the same depth of knowledge, passion or enthusiasm for your service as you can.

So the conversation might go like this:

You: Aside from you Anwar, is there anyone else involved in deciding which consultant to go with?

Anwar: Well, I make the final decision but it's my boss, Holly who has to approve the cost of anything I suggest.

You: Great, well at least that takes the pressure off you a bit, not having to worry about the pennies. It'd be really nice to get a chance to catch up with Holly and introduce myself, is she about today?

Anwar will either say, "Sure, I'll give her a ring and see if she can pop in". In which case this is a massive buying sign that he wants to buy because if he didn't then he sure as hell wouldn't waste Holly's time by suggesting she meet you.

He may also reply along these lines, "She's not about at the moment and anyway she will go with my recommendation".

This may or may not be true, however, accept it at face value and don't push further, simply make a note of Holly's name and position because she's going to become someone to try and meet, perhaps via a networking event.

** 'What kind of relationship do you ideally want from a consultant?'

This is a very touchy-feely question and one many people don't consider asking and yet it's an important one.

One organisation might wish for a really hands-on approach, one in which their preferred consultant will leave no stone unturned and work with everyone within the business.

Another might prefer something a little more hands-off, with only senior management being involved.

Some might want daily contact by telephone, another weekly via Zoom or Teams.

Never assume!

The questions detailed on the previous pages are there as a guide. You probably won't want to ask all of them because if you're listening properly, the answers you hear will prompt you to ask others, which you may not have even considered asking.

Take notes! As soon as you ask the first question, always ask if they mind if you take notes.

Taking notes allows you to recall what you discussed at a later date, prompts you to ask others and is a very clear indication to your prospect that you are genuinely interested in what they are saying.

Listen to their answers and watch out for opportunities to ask for business or at least move the conversation towards getting business.

It would be impossible for us to attempt to list all the many varied ways in which a prospect may express an interest (often referred to as a 'buying sign' by salespeople) but here are a few.

- What do you charge? (If they weren't interested in what you had, they wouldn't care what you charged.)
- Can you come in in the evenings?

What similar organisations have you helped/worked with?

- Have you ever done…?
- Would you consider…?
- I'd like you to meet our head of…?

All these are questions that would not ordinarily asked if the prospect was not interested.

> WARNING
>
> There is a phenomenon in sales which is referred to as 'Selling yourself in and selling yourself out' and it's a blight often visited by the less experienced. Be aware of it!

What happens is you explain all about the services and ways you can help, and the client says 'Yes' or gives a more subtle buying sign but rather than stopping and securing commitment, you continue explaining more about what else you do because you 'must' finish your entire pitch!

Meanwhile, the prospect hears something you say in your additional spiel, which causes them to have second thoughts or sows a seed of doubt, and when you finally ask for the business and shut up, they say they had better think about it and on reflection, have a word with the Finance Director.

Bugger!

Again, it's about listening not simply information gathering. Salespeople are always moving the conversation forward, looking out for opportunities to close the deal/get commitment.

Features and Benefits

This must be one of the first topics any budding salesperson learns about: the difference between benefits and features.

At some point in this meeting, you are going to need to tell your potential client about what service you provide, the sorts of organisations and the kinds of projects with which you are currently involved.

However, what you tell this person will be dictated by the information you have gleaned from the questions you asked.

Letting a prospect know you have 30 years of experience in the hotel and leisure sector or have helped umpteen SMEs embed a superb culture, are features: whilst they may seem exciting to you, they might be of no consequence whatsoever to the person seated in front of you.

In fact, imagine them saying to themselves 'So what?'

What you need to do is tell them the benefit of your experience. In other words, 'which means that…'

'I have over 30 years of experience in the hotel and leisure sector (feature)…which means that you can rest assured I have witnessed most problems experienced by the front of house teams and have tried and tested solutions to their problems, and, more importantly, talk their language'.

You MUST emphasise the benefit to the prospect!

Extolling the features of your offering is great: keep doing it. However, always back it up with a benefit!

Wants and Needs

A Definition

Wants are expressed, whereas needs are the desires and wishes that lie behind those expressed wants.

Any easy illustration explains the difference.

You are meeting a prospect and they tell you they WANT to cut their annual recruitment budget by 10%.

The conversation with them continues, during which it comes to light they have a new boss, from whom this new instruction has emanated and they now have to report recruitment figures every other month, as opposed to annually, which was the case with their previous manager.

Further information is revealed regarding how, over the past few years, the business had lost a number of staff and found it to be increasingly difficult to recruit replacements.

In this case, the want has been stated explicitly – a desire to slash 10% from recruitment. However, what you have perhaps also been given an insight into is the NEEDS underlying this. WANTS are always the expressed desire in the pursuit of satisfying a NEED or NEEDS.

It would appear your prospect's needs are for a quiet life (no hassle from the boss, every other month) to impress them (they are new in the post) and to show they have value to the organisation (they can knock 10% off the bottom line).

The point in ascertaining the difference between wants and needs is that there is only ONE way to satisfy the former – to make it happen – in this case to log a figure in a spreadsheet, next to 'recruitment', which is 10% lower than last year's.

Although there may be other ways to satisfy 'NEEDS', there are alternative ways in which you could assist your prospect in looking good in front of their boss. There will be other avenues from which 10% might be saved.

Understand that 'NEEDS' can open up a wider range of solutions!

The key, therefore, is to listen intently. Your prospect will come right out and tell you what they want, your job is to ask more questions, listen and uncover what it is that lies behind those wants: what do they really need?

Listen to what people are really saying. Do not accept their expressed 'wants' at face value. Sit back, ask more questions and find out what 'needs' lie behind them. And then seek to address those.

You've targeted, connected and met; now it's time to…

Chapter 5

Asking for the Business and Handling Objections

ASK (Stage Four)

Asking for the business is what some term as 'closing' or 'sealing the deal', both of which can sometimes have rather negative connotations – images of pushy sales people, deploying sneaky, underhand tactics and ploys to part good, honest people from their money!

Here at Tricres, we prefer 'Ask'. It's softer, gently and less salesy!

This is THE most important aspect of the business development process because everything you have done has been leading up to this point.

Example

Nick went to see the Global Head of Learning and Development of a global, professional services firm. Towards the end of the meeting, he asked her if there was any work he could do for them right away and if there wasn't, what was the best way to go about doing so in the future?

The prospect paused and answered in the affirmative.

Nick then said he hoped she hadn't minded him being so direct. To which she gave a very telling response:

"I'd have been disappointed if you hadn't asked".

You MUST always ask for the potential client's business. For two reasons:

You need to know where you stand – are these people ready to buy or are they not?

The prospect is expecting you to!

When Nick had telephoned the prospect and secured a date in her diary and travelled from Edinburgh to London, they knew why he had done so: because he wanted her firm to use his services!

When you follow up after a networking event, take someone for a coffee, invite them out for lunch or secure a date in their diary to pop in and see

DOI: 10.4324/9781003602422-5

them at their offices, they do know the reason why! It is NOT a shock you want them to buy something!

It's analogous to a 'courtship' with a potential romantic partner.

There is a initial connection, meeting, conversation and hopefully, first date. If the relationship is going to progress, however, someone is going to have to lean in an attempt to kiss the other!

If this doesn't happen, the relationship remains 'stuck'. Many people in business, with whom we have worked have become stuck, in what we refer to as the 'never-ending courtship'!

Consultants and coaches take potential clients out for umpteen coffees, and lunches, inviting them to networking events, etc., and NEVER, actually make it clear they would like to work with them, by asking for the work!

As a person in business you can wine and dine your prospective clients as much as you wish but there comes a point where you have to do the business equivalent of going for the kiss – ask for their business. And you do this for the same reason as you would in a potentially romantic relationship. You cannot afford to be spending time courting someone who takes your hospitality but gives their business to a rival.

Sure, keep in touch, don't let them off your radar but if they are happy with their current supplier one sure way of finding out if that's the case is asking them to do business with you. Because it's at that point they will let you know unequivocally that they intend to remain faithful – at least for the time being. And here is where business relationships differ from romantic. A business relationship is never for life: organisations do change suppliers and neither are they monogamous – they are quite often up for a bit on the side so they can sample what else is out there and ditch who they have right now – should their current supplier ever take them for granted.

Message – wine and dine all you want but at some point, you've got to go for the kiss – ASK for their business. In other words: get COMMITMENT.

The Use of Silence

Once you've asked for the business, which might go like this:

- "It's been great having a coffee and learning about your business, of course, I'd love to work with you and the team and think we could work well together; how do we go about doing that?"
- "The feedback from the last session was really good. I'd love to do more work with you, what else can I help you with?"
- "Ok, you say you are looking to work with a coach/consultant or at least reviewing the situation later in the year. It goes without saying I'd love to be considered, when do I need to make our formal submission?" Or "How's best to go about being considered?"

Once you have asked. Once you have posed a question similar to any of the above, STOP TALKING.

Silence is the single most powerful way to get a commitment.

We don't like silences: they're awkward. When there is one, we are tempted to fill it – with more talk.

Well, that's fine when you have just asked for the business, just as long as it's not you that fills it! You shut up, look them in the eye and wait!

And this is true when you are asking for the business as it is when you are making an appointment to see someone – "So, is the 4th or 5th best for you?" "The morning or the afternoon of the 18th?" ask the question and then say nothing.

We can't stress how important asking for the business is. Few people do this. Even those experienced in sales forget on occasion but it's rampant among those who are from professions and sectors where business development is a relatively new thing.

Many of these people have got into a mindset where they think that if they invite people to sufficient networking events, take them to enough sports fixtures, play sufficient rounds of golf, get them to attend enough seminars and receive an inbox load of e-newsletters, that they will eventually win work: a kind of developing business by smothering people in BD process.

Example

A few years back Nick was having a chat with the CEO of a law firm in the Midlands.

He told him a major PLC had been wooing and courting him over the past two years. As part of this courtship he and his wife had been guests of the organisation at the Cheltenham Festival – twice. Had been taken to London to have a grandstand view of the London marathon, which was followed by a cookery lesson given by a leading chef and all topped off with a slap-up meal at said chef's restaurant.

When Nick commented on how lucky he was to have had such corporate entertainment lavished upon him, the CEO paused and said, "Yes, but do you know what, no one from the organisation has yet approached me and asked for my business and to be honest I haven't a clue what it is they want exactly".

There is another reason why you should ask for the business: it can often rival objections!

Handling Objections

Objections are the reasons prospects will give you for not buying.

They are like blockages in a pipe or a fallen tree across a road: they are in the way of your desired destination.

When you first hear an objection it's tempting to become defensive or become disheartened and pretend it doesn't matter.

First things first: when it comes to objections, if you are getting them it's because your prospect doesn't understand the value of what it is you have to offer. In other words, you haven't done your job properly.

When it comes to dealing with objections, prevention is better than cure. Inoculate your potential client against them!

You should know the strengths and weaknesses of your offering and be aware of the possible objections you may expect to hear and address them before a prospect brings them up.

Example

You are a sole trader or working alone under the banner of a limited company. You are aware your potential client could well be talking to other, potential providers, many of whom are bigger than yours and can lead with a number of experienced coaches and consultants.

When they ask you to tell them more about you and your 'organisation' you may be tempted to try and 'big yourself up', because you're aware of the downside of being 'small'.

Don't! Turn it into a positive AND knock the potential objection on the head!

"Well, the company is just me, is only ever going to be me. One of the reasons my clients say they like working with me, is because they only have one point of contact. I'm the person who sits down and works out what the business needs, I am the person everyone sees and works within the organisation. I'm the single point of contact, meaning everyone only has to deal with me. It's me they build the relationship with, which builds comfort and trust. And, because there's only me, I don't have the big overhead of the larger consultancies, which means my clients often pay less".

No matter how much you inoculate prospects against 'catching' objections, they will, inevitably, arise.

What if they come up?

First of all, relax. Acknowledge the objection, discover more about why the issue has been raised, what's worrying them and the deal with it.

You mustn't take objections at face value and simply counter them with a quick but polite riposte.

An objection might be phrased like this:

Tiffany: Well, Nick, what you say sounds great and on principle I am happy to use your services, however, I'm a little concerned that you are more expensive than the other quotes I've received.

The first thing to note here is that Nick has been thorough in his questioning, he would know that she had obtained other quotes and – if she'd been willing to tell him – from which of his competitors. With his knowledge of the market, Nick should know roughly how much they would be charging.

So, when faced with the old "it's too expensive", Nick should avoid the temptation to contradict – which is an easy trap within which to fall.

Nick: I like to think my price reflects the current market rate. Or Well our research tells us that we are competitively priced.

Both of which are simply a terribly polite way of saying 'No we are not!"

Here's what Nick should do!

Accept the objection.

Nick: Ok, price is a concern for you.
He should then write this down! Writing it down lets Tiffany know he takes her concern seriously.

Nick: Is there anything else that concerns you about using me?
He is being upfront here. He might be scared to know this because what if Tiffany trots out an entire list of reasons? Well, what if she does? At least he'll know what hurdles he needs to get over.
Don't be afraid to ask if there's anything else. And get everything out in the open.

Tiffany: Yes, I'm a little concerned you are based so far from London.

Nick: OK (*He writes this down – the objection, not the word 'OK'*).

Tiffany: No.

Nick: Sure?

"OK. If I can provide assurance as to these two things, would you feel comfortable to go ahead?"

Now, this is a cracking line and sorts the pros from the amateurs in developing business. What Nick has done here is use an objection as an opportunity to get a commitment.

This is sales ballet – elegant, yet powerful – and it moves him closer to a sale because he now knows that all he has to do is address those two concerns and Tiffany has told him she'll buy from him.

Let's just take one of those concerns – geographical location.

Tiffany has let him know she is concerned he isn't London-based.

Now the secret here is for him to discover what lies behind the objection. Often you'll find that a stated objection, simply, masks the real issue and it is that with which he must discover.

Reasons why she might have said this:

- She would feel better if he was immediately available to pop into her office. Living out of London will surely incur travelling costs and possibly overnight accommodation expenses. Is she going to have to pay for those? How much will they be?
- She perceives London-based SMEs as experiencing challenges unique to that geographical area, with which Nick may not be up to speed. She would gain reassurance if she could see Nick's place of work.

In order to find out what the real worry is, Nick needs to ask the following:

Nick: I am curious what in particular concerns you about my location in Cheshire rather than London?

She may then list some of the above, which Nick can then deal with individually, replying along the following lines:

- I live ten minutes from the station, from where it's only two hours into London. Living that close means I can get to clients with short notice and get there and back in one day.
- I understand your thoughts about London being a 'bit different' and agree it does have some unique challenges. Thankfully, I have been helping firms in London for over 17 years now.

The really awkward one.

- "I'll think about it".

This is not really an objection but it is a phrase one hears a great deal!

First of all, as with any objection, ask them:

You: What is there in particular that you feel needs further thought? I'm concerned I have perhaps omitted to tell you something about how I might help that gives you the full picture.

Them: No, you have been very helpful and I feel I know everything I need to know. It's just that I like to give such matters some thought.

Don't push here! If you start to get too pushy, you're going to annoy them and all the work you've done to get to know them will have been wasted.

We all want to have time to think about purchasing decisions, so allow them!

Still, you want to keep control here and not simply leave them with the ball in their court. That being the case, here's what you say.

You: No problem. Of course, you want to think about it and I don't want to hassle you so I'll leave it with you. If I've not heard from you within 2/3 weeks, or 3/6 months, when shall I drop you a line to see where we're up to?

Example One

Nick was once in front of a prospect who said she wanted to think about things and her initial challenge was to persuade the management team soft skills training was important.

He told her he would leave it with her and wouldn't bother her again (people appreciate this because most people set on business development do pester) but did ask when he should next get in touch, before furnishing her with two options (the alternative close).

"In a couple of months or into the New Year?" to which she replied, "Give me a call in January".

They both knew where they stood and Nick had her permission to get in touch in January. She knew he would not bother her and equally he wasn't left wondering, whether, over the following few months, he should get in touch or leave it a little bit longer, which freed him up to concentrate on other potential clients for whom the timing might be better.

Example Two

Nick had a client with which he did loads of work, and the feedback was great. They lost touch for a year but a chance meeting on a train with one of the senior directors resulted in one piece of work, which he duly delivered.

There then was a period where Nick was asked to quote for a piece of work, right at the last minute, which he did but did not win.

As part of his focus on keeping in touch and going to see clients, he visited the head of training and her assistant. The meeting went well.

He asked if there was anything else he could help them with and there was a pause....which told him there was a problem: a blockage to business.

So, he asked them to tell him what was on their mind and they did. They were worried that he only did 'one thing'.

Client: I have seen you deliver training Nick and I'm worried that what I saw is all that you do. It was very good but only for those kinds of big audience gigs.

Nick: Ok, what worries you about that?

She expanded whilst he made a note and listened intently.

He then reminded the pair of them of all the other stuff he had done for the firm in the past, which were to groups of six to eight and had been on different topics. He also mentioned – referring to the names of clients she would recognise – other training sessions he'd delivered and the resulting feedback.

Nick: Is there anything else?

Client: Yes, when I called you to ask you to quote for that bit of work some months back I asked another provider as well and whereas they came to see me because they felt they needed to know more before putting a proposal together, you didn't. You just sent something over in writing.

Nick: That's true. Can I ask you what bothered you about that?

She told him she felt that in his eagerness to secure the work he'd cobbled something together and, in contrast to the other provider, felt that he'd had not put a lot of thought into it.

Nick reminded her that when she had asked for the quote and provided a training outline, she had said she needed it urgently. The reason he hadn't requested a meeting was to find out more about her requirements because ordinarily he would.

With everything out in the open Nick and his client were able to talk through their worries and he was able to address them.

He thanked them for being so honest and was glad they felt they could bring this to his attention.

What is amazing is they went on to say the only reason they felt comfortable expressing their views was because of the fantastic relationship they had with Nick. What's more – and this is the whole point around this – they went on to say they normally don't bother telling suppliers why they won't use them, because they can't be bothered but that such was their relationship, they felt it important!

Ten days later they asked him to quote for another big and important piece of work!

LESSON – find out what your potential client is worried about and deal with it!

A Final Point on Objections

Feel Felt Found

Your prospect: "I'm worried you don't have a great deal of experience in the haulage sector".

Your response:

> I know exactly how you FEEL. To be honest, you'll not be surprised to hear a number of my clients FELT exactly the same way prior to working with me but what they've FOUND is the experience I have of the materials handling sector has proved surprisingly beneficial.

Summary

Accept the objection. Find out what lies behind it – the real reason – and then address it.

Do this with each one in turn and check with the prospect whether they are comforted by your answer. If they're not, find out what is still bothering them and repeat the process.

Possible outcomes of meetings

- They love you and your suggestions of how you might help improve their business and want to do business with you.
- They love you and your offering but want to think about it/consult a colleague.
- They love you and your offering but are happy with their current consultant.
- They love you but aren't keen on what you're offering.
- They don't like you one little bit.

There must be loads of other possible outcomes to meetings but we reckon these five cover 99% of them.

- Great – get the ball rolling and secure the first date to come in a speak to the board or management team.
- No problem. If you have asked the right questions, you'll know who the colleague is and you'll have already asked about how you go about setting up a meeting with them.

  If it's someone you don't know or meeting them isn't possible, tell your contact that you will leave it with them but check when you should get in touch if you don't hear back from them in two/three weeks (use the alternative and make sure they see you make a note of the date in your diary.)
- Fine. If you have asked the right questions, you'll know when it's up for review and have asked them when you should next be in touch because 'I'd love to be considered for that'.

  Even if that's not an option – they aren't reviewing it in the foreseeable future – let them know you'll not bother them and drop them off sometime in the future to see if your timing's better.
- Acknowledge the fact that you can't help them. If you feel comfortable, ask if they know anyone who would be interested in what you are offering or ask them what kind of related services they may find helpful and, if it's possible, start supplying them!
- Shake their hand. Thank them for their time and when you are far enough away, mutter "NEXT", under your breath.

Having a 'style'

You cannot have got this far and not realise it is YOU people are going to buy.

And given that is the case, it is essential 'you' come across when you CONNECT and MEET with people.

We've furnished you with lots of examples; sufficient that you should have a very clear sense of our character, personality and style.

In fact, you should have been able to get a very good sense of that even if we had not bothered including examples of the letters and emails: the book should speak loudly enough in the way it is written.

Being 'you', being authentic, should be the easiest thing in the world but when put in 'work mode' we all tend to wear a 'mask' and whilst you cannot behave in the world of work as you do with your mates or at home, if you are to have success in developing business, then you must allow people to see you minus the disguise.

For some of you, it'll take a while until you feel comfortable with this idea, for others, a blessed relief to ditch that fake persona you've been under the impression you had to adopt.

You must develop your own style. You aren't Nick Davies or Rebecca Bonnington.

Far too many people, in attempting to convey a professional image just end up coming across as terribly earnest. They attempt to be ALL things to ALL people, which results in them being nothing to everyone!

It is quite possible to be professional, earn people's trust and be seen as credible whilst still remaining essentially YOU!

In a world that seems intent, through social media, to shout 'LOOK AT ME' and with all the 'noise' we have created – the internet, LinkedIn, TikTok, Insta, FaceBook, email, WhatsApp, endless streaming services, YouTube and 24-hour rolling news – it's increasingly hard to stand and be noticed for the right reasons in the business world. But to stand out and be remembered, you must!

Be yourself.

As Oscar Wilde expressed so wisely: 'Be yourself; everyone else is already taken'.

A senior equity partner at a global financial services firm summed it up nicely recently.

> Nick, over the next 3 weeks, about 7 people will come into my office to see me. They will all get their laptop out and without really looking at me, run through a load of slides. I wish, just once, that someone would just come in and chew the fat with me.

Cut the crap, be yourself and win some business.

Chapter 6

Your Core Offering

Why Products Matter in Business Coaching and Consulting. This part is written by Rebecca. She Founded Tricres and created the models and frameworks our brilliant business coaches use with their clients.

If you recall, Chapter 2 featured the Economic Engine Model. This model talked about business consulting and coaching as a service-led business. Why, then, would we start talking about a product?

It's a good question.

You are running a business which is almost entirely focused on delivering a service to your clients. However, you need something that looks and feels like a product in order to get the conversation going with your prospective clients. Because services aren't physical things, it's often quite hard for clients to understand exactly what you can do for them. As humans, we like to make decisions based on our feelings and then rationalise those decisions later.

When you're selling a service, the client might love you and really want to work with you, but they need to be able to rationalise this feeling or explain what you can do for the business to their board of directors or other team members. This is virtually impossible to do without referring to a product.

Let me give you an example.

The owner of Client A Ltd knows they need some help in moving the business from a small team of 12 people with 1 office to a team of 20 with 2 offices. The owner realises there are systems, processes and ways of working they don't yet have knowledge of and they think getting a business coach and consultant will help them understand what their priorities and next steps should be.

So far, so good.

The business owner has two business partners she needs to discuss this with and keeps getting asked questions like 'What would a business coach say or do that we don't already know'. She's stuck as she's not sure what the answer to that question is.

DOI: 10.4324/9781003602422-6

If the business coach has discussed a 'product' with the business owner then she will know precisely what the business coach will be doing. I'll use the Tricres products to explain precisely how this works.

We talk with prospective clients about their businesses and gather lots of information. We then ask questions to find out what their biggest issues are. We categorise these issues into People, Revenue or Strategy issues. This is the first cornerstone of our product and helps clients get clarity on where the core issues sit in their business.

Once we know whether the key issues are in the People, Strategy or Revenue category, we can then drill down a bit more and find out what's going on. We know from decades of experience that it's likely to be one of the following:

- Can't get consistent profitable sales
- Can't find the right kind of people or retain them
- Not sure what direction to take the business

The issues can be dressed up in many different ways, but essentially these are the main ones you'll come across as a business coach.

We have developed over 22 models and frameworks (products) which make it very easy to answer these issues quickly. At our fingertips, we have bright, colourful images of those models (they're all very simple) that we can show to clients and talk them through the key principles.

The Economic Engine in Chapter 2 is one such model.

Instantly, the client understands what you're talking about, understands the process you'll take them through and most importantly has a solid, tangible 'thing' they can show their business partners and think about after their meeting with you.

Another such product in the Tricres toolkit is the 21st Century Leadership Programme. It's an eight-module leadership development programme which has its own glossy PDF brochure. It has a single-page PDF model that can be sent out or used very quickly to illustrate what's inside the product. See the model below.

I'm hoping by now you can see and feel how much easier it is to 'sell' what you do by using a product. I've put 'sell' in parenthesis because you're not selling anything, you're asking great questions and responding with answers.

Finally, having products gives you something to put on your website, makes it easier to deliver talks and helps you shape your offering so people know what you can deliver for them. Coaching and consulting are often labelled as 'soft' or not viewed as having tangible results. Having products gives you a start and a finishing point which means you can measure a 'before' and 'after' effect.

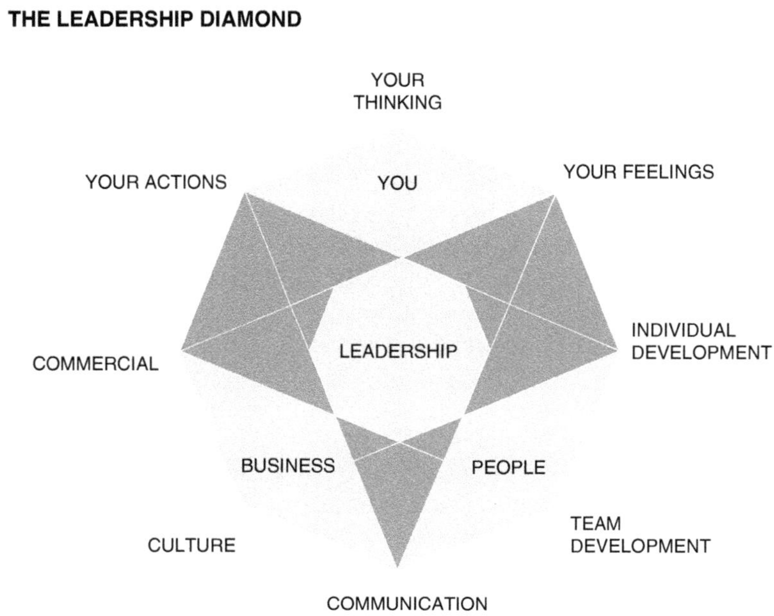

Figure 6.1 The Leadership Diamond.

Don't make the mistake we did when we started Tricres. We started with 18 products and attempted to bundle them up into one big product. No one understood what we were doing and no one bought anything.

Start with one core product and build from there. We now have 20 products but have learned how to wrap them up into bitesize chunks and create three core products. It's only been five years!

Here are our current core products:

- Kick A** Culture Coach and Consultant Training (this contains all our programmes in one big product)
- NLP for Business Coaches
- Business Development for Business Coaches

What we should have done and what I'd advise you to do, is start with something small and simple and then build from there. We did it backwards and I would not recommend that!

If you want to learn more about our products visit www.tricres.com

Here are a couple of stories from our founders about opportunities and new content.

Nick's Story

'Better Never Stops' was a phrase first coined by Sir Dave Brailsford, the former performance coach of the British Cycling team.

And it's as true for coaches and consultants.

As it is for pedalling quickly around a velodrome.

Continuing professional development is your responsibility when you work for yourself and it has a couple of clear benefits:

It keeps you up to date with what's going on in your sector and area of expertise and, as a result, maintains your credibility with clients and prospects. It sparks ideas, which can lead to you developing new models and enhancing existing ones.

The Lockdown in spring 2020 was, for the self-employed, a very difficult time. (We speak from experience!)

However, as Gandhi said, 'Adversity is the mother of progress'.

Even as restrictions were eased, it became clear that communicating virtually via Teams and Zoom was not only here to stay but would play a large part in how people in business communicated.

Nick, whose specialist area is communication skills, set to work learning more about how human beings established and nurtured relationships and more importantly, which aspects of the process were compromised in the virtual world.

Eventually, he had enough information to formulate a 90-minute course/workshop, which he set about letting his clients know about: 'Establishing and Building Business Relationships in the Virtual World'.

This has now become a popular course with clients and one which is as in demand today as it was during the height of lockdown.

In addition to creating a stand-alone course, communicating virtually is an element now embedded in ALL the programmes Nick delivers.

Always keep your eyes and ears open for opportunities to enhance and add to your existing models and frameworks.

As Big Weld, the animated character in 'Robots' says, 'See a need, fill a need'.

Rebecca's Story

Rebecca has two stories to tell.

One is about 21st Century Leadership Programme and how it came into being and the other is about Strategic Thinking Made Easy.

A client of mine asked me if I could deliver leadership development for their team. They gave me a spreadsheet with the data they'd collected about where the gaps in their leadership team's skill set were.

I took that spreadsheet away and added some additional content to it. What I built from that was an eight-module leadership development programme which I then presented to the company's CEO. I quoted a delivery price and he went away to think about it.

Several weeks later he came back and gave me the go-ahead to deliver the programme to three layers of their leadership and management team over three days every two months.

At this point, I jumped up and down for joy and set about scheduling the dates and creating the agendas. It was a huge amount of work. I had to write all the workbooks, presentations and exercises for the groups from scratch. I had the content either in my head or had delivered certain parts of the content for other clients. I also had to come up with a name for it!

This was my first real product.

By meeting a client's need, spending time and money in creating something that looked and felt very high quality and delivering it in my usual honest and open style, I discovered I had a real hit on my hands.

The 21st Century Leadership Programme became a cornerstone of my coaching and consulting business and to date, I've delivered it about ten times to lots of different clients. It's kept my cash flow positive and reassured me that I've had at least 8 to 16 months' worth of income coming into my business.

All from saying 'yes' to a client.

The Strategic Thinking Made Easy course came about through a referral from another coach. A huge, multi-national business was seeking strategic thinking training for its leadership cohort.

The Head of Learning and Development (L&D) needed a two-hour session for 24 people. I'd never done anything like this before, but through a series of Teams calls I found out what the client wanted and most importantly what she wanted the people on the training to have learnt.

I put an agenda together and shared it with the Head of L&D. She loved it. I delivered it and afterwards, she said it was the best strategic thinking workshop she'd ever seen. I've been invited back again to deliver it to the next cohort of leaders.

I'm not showing off. What I want to illustrate is that your clients will tell you what they want and as long as it's within the range of your skills and knowledge, say 'yes' and then go away and create something.

If one client wants it, I guarantee other clients will want it too. Keep your eyes on the horizon, notice what clients are asking about and deliver sessions that answer those questions.

Chapter 7

What Should I Charge?

How Much Do I Charge?

The price you charge clients can often be tricky for some: many people have a reluctance to talk about money.

However, talk about money, you must because you have bills to pay and financial commitments to meet. Money may not buy happiness but once it's sorted, it frees you up to worry about the other stuff!

There are a number of things to say about charging and fees. The first is this…

'Be proud of your price!'

You should not be embarrassed about how much you charge.

You wouldn't walk into a Rolex dealership, enquire as to how much a watch was, only have the salesperson blush and rather embarrassingly, declare…

'It's 9000 pounds. Yes, I know! It's an awful lot for something your phone does anyway, and to be honest, more accurately! I have emailed management in Switzerland and told them our watches are really very costly given they do the same thing as those costing a hundredth of the cost. And then there's the price of insurance and the worry it might get stolen or damaged…'

You get the picture!

Second, whilst you may charge by the day, that's not what your client is paying for! They are paying for the countless years of studying, reading and hands-on experience you have accrued.

Lawyers charge by the hour, which can, at first glance, seem terribly overpriced but remember what you are really paying for – what they have had to do to get to that point.

Talking about Money

Our advice is to bring up the subject of fees as soon as you can, rather than trying to avoid it.

DOI: 10.4324/9781003602422-7

One of the frustrations of selling services is expending lots of time on meeting a potential client, conducting a fact find and beginning to interview people, only to have your first invoice queried because there was a misunderstanding between you and the client.

Far better to have a discussion upfront about money and not secure the assignment, than to waste countless time and effort, only to arrive at a point where your invoice is queried and you end up working for virtually nothing!

Beware of Giving It Away

When working for someone else, doing stuff for free on the promise of paid work in the future is no big deal. It is when you work for yourself!

The 'carrot' of lots of work, if you agree to do something for free, is a seductive one and we'd not rule it out totally. However, in our many decades of experience, these promises of future, lucrative work rarely, if EVER, materialise!

If you are going to do something for 'free' because it will allow you to prove to your fledgling client how good you are, perhaps set it up like this…

"I will deliver an introductory 3-hour workshop to your board for my usual fee of £1995 + VAT, which I will then deduct from any subsequent work you put my way".

In this way, they get to see you in action and witness the value you bring, whilst you maintain your professionalism, dignity and ability to pay next month's bills!

Another couple of points to bear in mind before being tempted to offer anything for free or give away for a huge discount:

The client doesn't put a value on what you do because you've given it away. It's harder to go back and charge your full, 'proper' rate because your initial discount was so generous. The bottom line is, whether you wish to be the Ryanair or Emirates of business coaching and consultancy!

Both have their pros and cons.

If you are 'Ryanair' – cheap and cheerful, you will undoubtedly get lots of work and always be busy.

Emirates – less work but if you do win, will pay well.

There is always a trade and as clients know – as we all do – you get what you pay for!

Throughout this book, we've talked about charging for value and not for time. Clients are paying you for decades of experience or specialist knowledge and expertise. You cannot put a time limit on that. The best-paid coaches and consultants charge based on what they deliver. They do not charge day rates or hourly rates. This is an outdated and old-fashioned way of doing business. We understand lawyers charge every six to ten minutes for their time, however, even this model is changing slowly.

With the advent of increasingly sophisticated AI systems, getting an answer to a question is easy. Anyone can do that. What clients want is an interpretation of an answer, questions about their thinking and alternative scenarios put forward. AI doesn't do this yet. It might one day, but not yet.

What clients also want is a human. Running a business is very difficult. It's not getting any easier. Managing the rapid pace of change, shifting populations and changes in technology are the things that keep most business leaders awake at night. Only another human with the ability to listen, understand and probe is going to give those leaders the emotional and intellectual support they need to succeed.

That's where you come in. This is not a commodity. It can never be commoditised (despite our section on products – remember you're a service-led business with some products!) and that has a real value for business leaders. If someone asks you what your hourly rate is, say this, "I charge for value, not for time. A session with me costs a minimum of $500–$10,000" – you decide on your pricing structure depending on your experience, client base and demand for your services).

At this point, if the client is interested, they'll ask further questions about what a session consists of and what they might get out of it.

For longer-term relationships, we like to offer clients a couple of projects that need working on. We describe those projects give them the expected outcomes and then let them know how long we think it will take to deliver. When I'm doing this with clients, I work out what resources they have to commit to doing the work and what time I have available to support them.

It takes around six months to two years to create a purpose, vision and values and embed the behaviours and systems across the business. Depending on the size of the client and the people they have to deliver what is needed on the ground, determines how often I see them.

Here are a couple of examples.

One client has an exceptionally talented team who have been busy embedding the behaviours of the purpose, vision and values work I did with the board of directors. I saw them every two months at the start and now we're nearly at the end of the project, I see them every quarter for an hour. I charged them more at the start because there was more work and now charge them my minimum fee.

Another client I see one-to-one every quarter because she's so busy and I charge her above my minimum fee because I'm doing quite a lot of thinking for her.

Finally, I have another client for whom I charge several thousand a month because I attend various meetings throughout the year, support the senior team on an ad-hoc basis and have delivered multiple leadership development programmes for them.

I don't charge any of my clients by the hour or by the day. I set up recurring invoices or invoices per session and leave it at that. No one quibbles my invoices and everyone feels they're getting huge value for money.

If you can get into this habit, then you'll have strong relationships with your clients and a good, solid cashflow in your business. As Nick says, keep developing business even when you're busy. Don't get too comfortable.

Negotiation Essentials

Negotiating or 'haggling' is part and parcel of business-life and takes on more importance when it's your income at stake – imagine having to negotiate your monthly salary each month!

The wonderful thing about negotiation us there are no rules. Well, apart from one.

That one 'rule' is, when it comes to making offers…

ALWAYS go first!

Yep! Unless you are woefully ill-informed, in other words, you have no idea as to the worth of what it is you are offering, you should always be the party to put the first number on the table.

The reason being is it acts like an 'anchor', in that it 'fixes' the price in your counterparty's mind, and is very difficult to shift it.

Allow us to demonstrate with an example to which we can all relate.

Car dealerships have their pre-owned stock, lined up, with the price of each vehicle displayed prominently in large figures on the windscreen.

The potential customer sees the price of £19,995, looks around the car, test drives it, likes it and wishes to buy it. They know they should haggle because that's what one is supposed to do.

They haggle and the salesperson agrees to knock £595 off and throw in some mats and a full tank of fuel.

The purchaser walks away delighted – new car, clean mats and more or less 600 quid less than advertised.

But, who decided where this negotiation should start? Yep, the seller! Great isn't it? The person selling the car dictates where any haggling will begin! Hurrah!

Of course what the potential purchaser should ask is: 'I am curious to know how you arrive at the price you have displayed?'

- But, no one does that.
- Making offers! GO FIRST!
- Giving a discount.
- DO NOT give a discount if you are not asked for one!

It is tempting to offer up a price for your fee, let's say £2,895 for a day and then immediately, say something along the lines of… 'but I'll reduce that to

£2,595' without your potential client having even mentioned the possibility of a discount!

Acting so precipitously, sends a couple of messages:

You don't even value what you do and don't think you're worth your fee. If you discounted that quickly, imagine how much lower I can push you!

There will, of course, be occasions when, after negotiation, you may feel a discount is appropriate. Fine. Don't immediately go for 10%!

Again, it's amazing how many people, when asked to reduce their fee, do so by 10%. What happened to the nine numbers between one and ten?! What's wrong with offering three or four and perhaps settling on five or six?

How to Reveal Your Fee

Whether you are telling your potential client what you will charge in person or via email (we would always recommend the former because you are better able to judge their reaction, which could well be non-verbally) you should always tell them what they are going to get for the money, rather than divulging the price and then going on to detail what's included.

It might look like this…

'My daily fee, which includes all the preparation, teleconferences, my return travel, accommodation, work booklets and materials, food, drink, taxis, etc., is £2895 + VAT per day'

If you tell them the price first, the likelihood is they will not hear/read what is included because they are still thinking about the number!

Bottom Lines and BATNAs

Bottom Line

This pair are fundamental to ALL negotiations and you should be aware of them because they are similar but different.

The best way to highlight peoples' attitudes to bottom lines is by way of an illustration:

You want to sell your property and, having had it valued by a property expert at somewhere between £500,000 and £550,000, you have it listed. You have decided you will not take less than £500,000. This represents your bottom line. A figure which you will most definitely not go below! Definitely!

A prospective buyer turns up, views your property and decides to buy.

They offer to transfer the money to you there and then begin the transaction. Just as they are about to press 'send', they realise they do not have that amount in their account and are short by £100 and can only muster £499,900.

Will you take it or wait for another buyer, if and when one comes along… who can pay right away?

For the sake of a hundred quid? No, not likely! You'll take it. And in doing so you admit, if only to yourself, that £500,000 was not your bottom line!

And that's the point. When you hear a client, or anyone else for that matter, declare their bottom line, feel free to ignore it because it isn't!

From your perspective, whilst having a bottom line will help prevent you from being taken advantage of during a negotiation by a far more powerful counter-party, you should be wary of becoming too wedded to it.

Research and countless practical examples demonstrate that in around 50% of circumstances, negotiators failed to claim extra value at the negotiating table because they were so fixated on their bottom line, they failed to see or hear, information, which came to light, that would have led to a more beneficial deal!

Be wary!

BATNA: Best Alternative to a Negotiated Agreement

You should NEVER enter a negotiation without one of these! It's negotiation #101 and no self-respecting negotiator would dream of doing otherwise.

Your BATNA is what you will do in the event of not being able to reach a negotiated agreement. You have to have a plan B or C and even D!

This alternative may be fantastic and anything better than that which you might achieve at the negotiating table – in which case, why negotiate?

On the other hand, it might be awful, a very poor second to that which you desire. In this case, it's really going to focus your mind on working hard to achieve a resolution via negotiation.

REVEALING YOUR BATNA

This is a factor you must give thought to. In some cases, it might be advantageous to be upfront with a prospective or existing client and let them know their business is not the only offer of potential work you have.

Appreciating you have other firms wanting your services will make them realise you are in demand and may miss out if they don't arrive at a decision promptly. Additionally, they can't afford to be too aggressive in securing a discount from you!

In other circumstances, however, you may wish to keep your cards close to your chest and not reveal any alternatives available to you.

Either way, it's something to always bear in mind and keep an eye on as negotiations proceed.

A BIT ABOUT MINDSET

If you have been paying attention, you'll have noticed, that at no point have I referred to the party with whom you are negotiating, as 'the other side'!

If you approach negotiations, viewing your counterparty (the correct phrase!) as 'the other side' or 'opposition' you are painting it as a contest to be won. Those entering into discussions with this outlook tend to be more defensive and focused solely on their position and outcomes.

A negotiation is not something to be 'won' it is arriving at a solution to a problem which satisfies, as much as possible, the interests and needs of both parties. It is about creating rather than distributing value.

Another factor, which helps promotes this more collaborative approach is the seating arrangements chosen for your negotiation.

Most people sit opposite one another, which merely emphasises the 'me' versus 'you' tone. Such seating is akin to many sporting competitions – football, tennis, basketball, etc. – the opponents, face one another.

Notice, also, that when seated opposite your counterparty, you quite literally have a different perspective to them and see things from a different/opposing point of view.

So, what if you don't sit opposite but next to, or if that feels a little too uncomfortable, at 90 degrees to them?

Any document or proposal you place in front of you is seen from more or less the same perspective. You both share the focus of attention, namely, on the proposal, rather than each other!

The mantra to which all professional negotiators seek to adhere is:

'Soft on the person, hard/focused on the problem'

This sounds simple but is sometimes far from easy to do, particularly if your counterparty has behaved in a way, suggested or proposed something you find objectionable or insulting.

The impasse – when negotiations stall or your counter refuses to negotiate.

First of all, allow us to state the obvious: it is not possible to make people negotiate! If your potential client repeatedly says 'no' to everything and anything you suggest and refuses to be forthcoming with any ideas of their own, there is nothing you can do about it, expect…of course…true to your BATNA!

However, there are a few techniques used by professional negotiators, available to us humble consultants and coaches.

G.R.I.T.: GRADUAL REDUCTION IN TENSION

Ordinarily, when one party in a negotiation asks for an amendment to the agreement, no matter how small or insignificant to the other, the other party should ALWAYS ask for something that improves the deal in their favour. This quid pro quo utilises the innate human desire to reciprocate (we talk more about this in the next chapter when we examine 'Influence and Persuasion').

However, what GRIT does is set aside the normal 'rule' to offer something in expectation you will get something in return and simply do it to reduce tension.

There will often be times during negotiations when it all becomes a little bit tense and either or both parties become frustrated, bordering on angry.

We NEVER make sensible decisions when experiencing these states, so sometimes you want to make a gesture during discussions which acts to reduce tension.

This gesture might well be conceding something which is of very little value to you, but your counterpart attaches great weight or value upon.

M.E.S.O.: MULTIPLE EQUIVALENT SIMULTANEOUS OFFERS

You are reasonably advanced in securing a new coaching client but there are a number of sticking points on a few matters. You continue to argue your point of view, supporting, defending and justifying the reasoning behind your proposal against the objections of potential clients.

What if you stopped taking that approach and instead offered up three proposals: A, B and C, all of equivalent value but different in other regards?

What if you offered these to your prospect and suggested they look at all three and said which they preferred, was closer to meeting their needs and satisfying their interests?

Doing this gets them involved! They are no longer faced with one proposal but three (no more than three otherwise it's too much choice and harder for them to reach a decision).

Even if they reject A and C, dismissing them almost immediately, but hang on to B, saying 'Well, this is far from ideal but is better than the other 2!' – you have learned something AND you've got them engaged.

Invite Criticism

This approach to freeing up blockages is totally counterintuitive!

As mentioned when talking about option 2 – MESO – your natural approach is to 'sell' your proposal, justify and explain why you believe it to be rational and sensible and if your counterparty, attacks it, to defend it.

Inviting criticism is the opposite of that 'normal' approach.

In this scenario, you hand your proposal to your counterparty and ask them to delete and amend it as they see fit!

Once they've 'drafted' the agreement the way they'd like it, you return the favour and amend and delete the changes they made.

Once done, you pass it back and so on and so forth.

This powerful technique was used to give birth to the 'Camp David Agreement' signed by Egypt and Israel in 1978, in which both parties agreed to live peaceably and for the latter to hand over territory it had captured during the six-day war in 1967.

The document went backwards and forwards 22 times between the parties until a form of words emerged to which the presidents of both countries felt comfortable putting their signatures to.

SCAN ME

Figure 7.1 Business Development for Business Coaches, Includes the Negotiation Course QR Code.

Chapter 8

Building Relationships

Rebecca now guides you through the process of securing projects and retainers.

I've already talked a lot about charging for value and not for time. I've also talked about products and the programmes I've created which can be delivered over months as well as charging per project.

These are the elements you need to have in your coaching and consulting business so you can charge retainers and charge for projects.

There are two rules I have about charging retainers and for projects. You can adopt them or not, it's up to you.

Rule One

I don't have contracts. I don't believe in them for this kind of work. If you and your client have to refer to a contract, then the relationship has already broken down and you need to walk away.

My clients spend huge amounts of money with me because I don't tie them into a contract. They never feel resentful about paying my invoices because I only send them when I deliver work for them and I agree on the delivery timescales up front. I also give them an update note after each session so everyone can see the progress being made and what we've agreed to do.

Rule Two

The other rule I have is this: I only work with clients when I can see they're getting true value from that work. The second there is no value, I let them know I think they can manage on their own and let them get on with it.

This builds huge trust, gets me referrals and allows me to deliver what's needed for businesses when they need it. So many other business coaching and consulting models tie clients into expensive contracts which last much longer

DOI: 10.4324/9781003602422-8

than the value they've received. It happened to me as a business owner and I resented every penny I paid above and beyond the additional value I'd had.

Don't be greedy and think you can keep clients on a dripping tap. It will come back and bite you. Do what Nanny McFee does in the film of the same name, or Mary Poppins, be there whilst the business and the client need you, build the skills into the business and people and then leave them to get on with it. Be there when they grow and need you again and keep in touch. It's the most powerful thing you can do as a business coach and consultant.

The way I work retainers out is as follows:

I carry out the initial Fact Find, for which I charge a one-off fee. This allows the client to see my work in action and to get to know me. The clients know this is a one-off piece of work and understand they can take the Fact Find Report (I always present it to them in person) and implement the findings and recommendations themselves or they can engage me to support them to do this.

The client is not scared of being tied into contracts or agreements they can't get out of later. This makes them much more likely to engage you for the first piece of work.

At the end of the Report and Recommendations, I suggest two projects. These tackle the immediate issues in the business. I price each one with a total amount and then an option to pay over several months. I take a well-educated guess as to how long it's going to take me to implement the recommendations and divide that by the total amount I've quoted.

For example:

- The business lacks a clear vision and doesn't have clarity on direction or a clear, identifiable culture.

I would recommend a Purpose, Vision and Values workshop and state my price. For teams of six or more, I allow a full day. Any less, and it's half a day.

- The business doesn't have the right people working in the right roles in the right way.

I would recommend conducting a session around Players on The Pitch (it's a Tricres Model). Again, depending on the number of people you need to work with on this, I quote a half or full day.

Both of these projects need follow-up work. Once I've delivered the first workshop, I then recommend the follow-up work and that can take months!

When you take baby steps you don't frighten the client with a large quote that seems out of reach. It also gives the client time to value what you do and to manage their cash flow. It manages your cash flow too. The vast majority of my client interactions involve a retainer of some kind.

Influencing and Persuading

> Persuasion is the art of getting someone to do something they wouldn't ordinarily do if you didn't ask.
>
> Aristotle

Getting good at being able to influence and persuade effectively is going to help you become a more effective coach and consultant. Developing business will be easier and smoother, you will enter negotiations more confidently and you'll be a more decisive and effective manager.

Here's the good news: you are already great at it! You are influencing and persuading friends and family all the time and don't give it a moment's thought. BUT, you are probably not as effective when it comes to matters of a commercial nature, in a business setting.

There tend to be four mistakes people make when attempting to 'nudge' people, which are...

- They regard it as a single event rather than a process.
- They adopt an aggressive or slightly too assertive demeanour.
- They rely far too heavily on logic and fail to appreciate the importance emotions play.
- They seek to satisfy wants rather than addressing underlying needs.

This is a fascinating and absorbing subject, one that we have only relatively recently begun to fully understand.

However, we suggest the following if you are eager to learn more:

- 'Inside the Nudge Unit' – David Halpern
- 'Nudge' – Thaler and Sunstein
- 'Influence: the Psychology of Persuasion' – Robert Cialdini
- 'Persuasion' – James Borg
- 'Flipnosis' – Kevin Dutton

Ok, taking a look at the four mistakes.

Children are masters at influencing and persuading because they do it naturally, by instinct: they haven't learned any bad habits and they don't overthink it.

They know if you want something on Christmas Day, the 25th of December, you don't ask mum and dad two weeks prior to the big day! No! You begin sowing the seeds, dropping hints months in advance!

It is understandable people are wont to adopt an assertive approach and deluge the other party with information, facts and figures as to why they should be persuaded to take a particular course of action – because they don't know when they are going to get another opportunity!

However, once you realise it's a process it removes the pressure to go in 'all guns blazing'. Plus, people cannot absorb huge amount of information. The temptation is to take a 'belt and braces' approach, 'I HAVE to tell them EVERY REASON why they should be persuaded!'

The Two Vital Ingredients

If the delegates are to have any hope of mastering these skills, they must understand the two vital ingredients:

- Trust
- Credibility

Trust was something we looked at earlier in the book, about the 'Relationship Triangle'.

Your reputation is the single most important 'possession' you own, particularly as a professional advisor. Once trust is lost, it is very difficult to get it back.

You will earn trust by doing what you say you would do, turning up on time, getting back to people, etc. We know this is obvious but it's incredible how few people actually hold themselves to such standards.

Credibility is, in the main, something one acquires over time, as experience increases.

An airline captain possesses more credibility than that of the 'first officer' because they have been flying for longer: it can't be rushed. One has to be 'time-served'.

Of the two – trust and credibility, the former is the most important.

You could be regarded as THE most experienced business coach and consultant in your sector. You may have a host of letters after your name but if I don't trust you, it counts for nothing!

If you are to have any hope of influencing someone or persuading them to use your services, they have to feel as though you know what you're doing and can be trusted to help them.

A quick note on trust – your potential client will ALWAYS have to take a leap of faith.

They can read testimonials about you and have been recommended by friends to use you. Your profile on LinkedIn tells them you are experienced and your client list is impressive. They THINK they can trust you but it is not until you are actually working with them, they will know you can be trusted.

One of the authors mentioned earlier was Robert Cialdini.

It was he, through his extensive and exhaustive research, who discovered human being is influenced in six primary ways. These are…

- Likability
- Reciprocity
- Social proof
- Authority
- Consistency
- Scarcity

These are grouped in pairs because each pairing plays a specific role in the process of influencing.

- Let's take them in turn and then individually.
- Likability and Reciprocity act to establish the relationship.

Likability

We are far more influenced by those we like than by those we don't.

If you think about people with whom you have worked and been all happy to help, go out of your way to get things done for them, supported, etc., the chances are you did so because you liked them. You got on with them.

The opposite is true. We have all worked for managers or supervisors who have asked to complete a task, we've done so but to the minimum requirement, to avoid any hassle. You don't go out of your way for these people because you don't really warm to them.

Reciprocity

We are far more inclined to do something for someone who has done something for us. This need to reciprocate runs very deep with human beings and transcends culture and race.

There is an innate desire within us to 'keep the balance' and not be in debt to people. Not merely financially but 'socially'.

We all know when it's 'our turn' to have friends around or invite your child's friend over for a playdate or sleepover. Within a group of work colleagues or friends, we know who doesn't get a round of drinks in!

It is the powerful drive to reciprocate, which you should utilise when negotiating. If your counterparty asks you to amend a clause or term in your terms of business, which you are amenable to, use that moment to secure a reciprocal change, more favourable to you. Cialdini refers to this point in a 'transaction' as 'the golden moment' and one you should be at pains not to squander!

Adherence to the likability and reciprocal principle is as mentioned pretty much universal and why they 'establish the relationship'. They let each party know they are adhering to social and cultural norms which exist within relationships.

Of course, we have all met that occasional person who does NOT adhere to these: they are all take, take, take and seldom, if ever, give back. They are, thankfully, rare, which is why we always remember this person, even if it has been many years since we encountered them!

Social Proof and Authority seek to reassure the person you seek to influence, the decision they are about to make or have made, is the 'right' one.

If you were able to condense into one calendar year how long human beings have lived on earth, we lived in small communities, of not more than 150 until November 30th! Our brains evolved and were designed to communicate, face to face, outside, whilst in motion. Doing what the other members of the group did, or as the tribal elder advised, was in our interests and that innate, deep-seated desire remains.

Social Proof

Social proof is just a fancy way of saying 'What everybody else is doing'.

We are 'nudged' into buying that product on Amazon because 4,623 reviews amount to 5 stars. Trip Advisor works on the same basis: 'People like you made the same decision'.

The most obvious way this manifests itself in business is when your prospect enquires as to whether you have 'worked with any companies similar to ours?' Or asks 'Who else have you done work with?'

Why do they need to know? Are they not able to make an independent decision? The answer is 'No they are not!' Most of us need to know people before we have reached the same conclusion. It provides the comfort we seek.

Authority

When the 'crowd' is not there to provide comfort and reassurance to guide us in our decision-making, we are equally comforted by those we view as possessing authority.

This may be an individual who is AN authority on a particular subject and/or holds a position of authority. It could also be an authoritative source.

You might be having a hard time persuading your prospect to engage your services and find their reluctance is because, in their eyes, at least, you lack authority/knowledge on a subject. No problem, perhaps call on the services of a colleague or close friend who is and ask them to lead the discussions on that subject.

Alternatively, you might say, 'Don't take my word for it. Here's some research/an article by this person who is an authority'.

We have done just that over the preceding pages by drawing your attention to the fact that what we are telling you is from Robert Cialdini. One of THE leading authorities on this subject. Consistency and Scarcity seek to persuade the person you hope to influence, to take action.

Once you have got them to a point where they have been persuaded, there's one more step – to make them carry through on their promise.

Consistency (and Commitment) to Give It Its Full Title

This seeks to leverage the fact most people strive to be consistent: do what they said they would.

We all like to think of ourselves this way. People of our word, who can be relied upon to fulfil undertakings given. We do not like those who chop and change, who say one thing and do another. We view this as a rather poor characteristic and we certainly do not like the idea people may view us in that light.

One of the situations where this will be of help is when you hear a client say, 'Leave it with me'. Or 'I'll come back to you once I've had a word with Joseph'.

When next you encounter this, ask when you can expect to hear from them.

Joe: It's been interesting learning more about the services you offer and how you might be able to help the business. Leave it with me and I'll come back to you.

You: Sure. No problem at all. Happy to leave it with you and I'll not hassle you because it's not the way I work. However, if I've not heard back in two or three week/two or three months, when should I next get in touch?

Joe: Oh, I would be looking to come back to you before the end of the month.

You: Great! Well, I'll leave it with you and make a note in my diary to drop you a line/give you a ring in the second week of the following month.

You then make a note in your diary, in front of them or at least jot it down in your notebook.

Committing Joseph to a date when he will come back to you is not a guarantee he will. However, it increases, dramatically, the chances he will because he won't wish to be seen as inconsistent!

Similarly, you have told him what you will do and when. The meeting ended with both Joe and you knowing what's going to happen next. This is another point in the business development process, where you are keeping control and setting up the follow-up!

If you want to increase the chances Joseph will be true to his word, ask him – nice and casual – to confirm the next steps in an email.

Wish to really up the chances he will deliver? Ask him whilst other people are present.

Imagine you are in a meeting with four other people and you say you will have a proposal on their desks by 5.30 next Friday, in readiness for the next meeting.

Now imagine you are seated in that get-together and you have to confess you've not got a finished proposal with you. Look a bit daft, don't you?! Not a good look is it?

By the way, we use this need to be seen as consistent to make sure we deliver things on time. If a potential client asks us to get a proposal to them, without mentioning a time frame, we will impose our own. 'I'll have that to you by Thursday'. In doing so, we make sure we deliver – a day earlier if possible! Always underpromise and over-deliver. People love it!

Scarcity

We experience loss much more intensely than we do gain. It is this emotion we seek to 'nudge' others into taking action.

You see this all the time on airline and hotel booking sites: 'only two more seats available at this price and five other people are looking at these dates right now'.

Such a statement puts us under tremendous pressure to book there and then: to take action! And the airlines and hotels know this!

FOMO – or the Fear of Missing Out is a very real phenomenon. What's more, it lasts for longer!

If you were to find £200 in the pocket of a jacket you've worn for ages, you'd be delighted. However, contrast that feeling with realising you've lost or stolen £200 you withdrew from a cash machine. It's much more intense and what's more, in four, five, six weeks you are still annoyed. Whereas, that feeling of delight you experienced on finding that sum dissolved within a matter of 48 hours!

Leverage this innate feeling of people to nudge them into taking action. Not by telling them what they will gain by using your services, but rather by highlighting what they will lose if they don't! Tighten the pressure by alluding to the fact that not only will they miss out but a competitor will perhaps gain what they could have had.

This is what causes people to fight each other in crowded stores on the day the sale starts – not only might miss out on that last 80-inch screen TV, but the person next to them might get it!

Here are a couple of models or templates you can follow and have in mind when you next set out to influence and persuade.

The first S.P.I.C.E is taken from a wonderful book written by Professor Kevin Dutton, a research psychologist at Calleva Research Centre for Evolution and Human Science, University of Oxford.

S.P.I.C.E: A Simple Model to Follow (from 'Flipnosis' by Kevin Dutton)

- S – Simplicity
- P – Perceived self-interest
- I – Incongruity
- C – Confidence
- E – Empathy

Let's break this down.

Simplicity

Keep your message simple. Too much information and you can turn the other person off. They literally stop paying attention.

Multinationals and politicians do this all the time: try and condense what they are offering, what might want you to do, in as few words as possible and then repeat it:

- 'Make America Great Again' – Trump
- 'Yes we can' – Obama
- 'Hands Face Space' – the UK govt. during COVID
- 'Because you're worth it' – L'Oreal
- 'Just do it' – Nike

You get the picture.

Perceived Self-Interest

Appeal to their 'perceived self-interest'. Social proof and Authority and Scarcity and Consistency work because people believe or 'perceive' it as being in their interest to do what others are doing 'Social proof', behave as the professor of virology says you should, 'authority', book those last two airline seats before someone else does 'scarcity', etc.

However, it might NOT actually be in their interests. However, that's not their perception.

Incongruity

Doing something which gets the attention of others because it is unexpected or 'incongruent'.

For example, the temptation when attempting to secure a date in the diary with a potential client is to email them with 'Catch up' or 'Meet for a coffee?' Or 'How I can help your business' or something similar.

How many emails do you think this person receives each day? How many of them are sent by someone attempting to get a date in their diary?

How many sales emails do you receive? How many do you brother opening? Exactly!

The first thing you must do is 'persuade' the recipient to even open your email and your chances of success are limited if your email 'subject' is the same as lots of others!

Nick tends to prefer 'Tea and Cake' or 'Coffee and a sticky bun' in his subject title. The oddest and most incongruent has to be…

Tony Wilson: 'We do things differently here'.

And 'yes' the guy who received it – who had no knowledge of Nick – replied and suggested dates when they might meet up!

Confidence

You have to be confident in manner and word if you are to stand a chance of influencing or persuading someone.

Not arrogant! Confident.

We can tell when someone is not confident when they lack conviction or belief in what they are suggesting. It's one of the reasons, we said earlier on, you should be 'Proud of Your Price'.

Empathy

You know what you want to achieve. You are acutely aware and what you seek to presume them to do, but what is it going to feel like from their perspective? Who are they going have to justify any decision they make, to? You want to hear 'yes' but it may be hard for them to say it and deliver.

Understanding what the situation looks like and feels like – as best you are able – will help you influence and persuade because you are better equipped to frame things in a manner which makes it easy for them to 'buy'.

M.I.N.D.S.P.A.C.E.

This lovely phrase is the methodology created by the United Kingdom's Cabinet Office, for all government departments to follow when seeking to 'nudge' sections of society.

It's easy to understand and remember. Here are its elements:

- M – Messenger. It matters who conveys the message. People are more readily persuaded by those in authority, people we like or regard as experts.
- I – Incentives. We tend to act if it will bring us pleasure or enable us to avoid pain.

- N – Norms. We are more likely to comply if the request seems popular.
- D – Defaults. We tend to do what's easiest and stick with the status quo.
- S – Salience. We will act on what is in front of us, whatever is visible. What is in focus, we perceive as being causal.
- P – Priming. Our behaviour can be influenced by subtle cues, often, of which we are not even aware.
- A – Affect. We tend to act on emotion, rather than logic.
- C – Commitments. We endeavour to keep our obligations and be consistent in our habits.
- E – Ego. We do things that will improve our social status and foster an identity.

Where we are both up to and what have we learned?

Final Thoughts

The hardest part is getting started and, by the way, there is never an ideal time to begin being your own boss.

It's very easy to put things off by telling yourself that if the economy was better, interest rates were lower, the kids were no longer in school, we lived in a bigger house/different part of the country.

Let's be honest, if you are waiting for the ideal conditions before going it alone, you will never do it because such conditions have never existed.

A client remarked to me recently that 'we are not making any decisions on training at the moment until there's a bit more certainty'.

Really?!

Please pick a date in history when you knew for certain what was going to happen the next day.

Again, if you are waiting for certainty, you aren't going self-employed.

Once the decision is made, you have to go all in! There are no half-measures. Going all in means you are committed and HAVE to make it work: there's no turning back.

Sure, there are merits in attempting to establish your fledgling consultancy business alongside your 'proper' job but I rather think you'll end up doing neither particularly well. A lion cannot chase two gazelles. She's got to select one and pursue it relentlessly.

Take Massive Action

Whether you decide business coaching is your side hustle or you main job or whether you're employed in professional services, the one thing you have to do to develop business is to take massive action.

No one will ever buy anything from you unless and until you take action. If this still scares you after reading this book, you need to get in touch because Rebecca can use her NLP skills to clear that fear and get you started.

The rest of you need to put this book down and get started. NOW!

Thanks for taking the time to buy this and then read it. You're one of the few people who will get to the end and there will be even fewer who implement what we've outlined. You are the people who will succeed. Let us know how you get on at hello@tricres.com. Good luck.

Rebecca and Nick, Sister and Brother Writing Team

Figure 8.1 Business Development for Business Coaches Course QR Code.

Index

Note: *Italic* page numbers refer to figures.

www.ingramcontent.com/pod-product-compliance
Ingram Content Group UK Ltd.
Pitfield, Milton Keynes, MK11 3LW, UK
UKHW021946150925
462951UK00006B/119
* 9 7 8 1 0 3 2 9 9 1 2 0 7 *